Real Influence

Real Influence

PERSUADE WITHOUT PUSHING AND GAIN WITHOUT GIVING IN

Mark Goulston and John Ullmen

FOREWORD BY KEITH FERRAZZI

⊧AMACOM

American Management Association

New York • Atlanta • Brussels • Chicago • Mexico City • San Francisco
Shanghai • Tokyo • Toronto • Washington, D.C.

Bulk discounts available. For details visit:
www.amacombooks.org/go/specialsales
Or contact special sales:
Phone: 800-250-5308
E-mail: specialsls@amanet.org
View all the AMACOM titles at: www.amacombooks.org

This publication is designed to provide accurate and authoritative information in regard to the subject matter covered. It is sold with the understanding that the publisher is not engaged in rendering legal, accounting, or other professional service. If legal advice or other expert assistance is required, the services of a competent professional person should be sought.

Library of Congress Cataloging-in-Publication Data

Goulston, Mark.
  Real influence : persuade without pushing and gain without giving in /
Mark Goulston and John Ullmen ; foreword by Keith Ferrazzi.
     p. cm.
  Includes index.
  ISBN-13: 978-0-8144-2015-7 (hbk.)
  ISBN-10: 0-8144-2015-X (hbk.)
  1. Persuasion (Psychology) in organizations.   2. Communication in management—
Psychological aspects.   I. Ullmen, John B., 1966–   II. Title.
  HD30.3.G68 2012
  658.4'5—dc23
                                                                    2012035931

About AMA
American Management Association (www.amanet.org) is a world leader in talent development, advancing the skills of individuals to drive business success. Our mission is to support the goals of individuals and organizations through a complete range of products and services, including classroom and virtual seminars, webcasts, webinars, podcasts, conferences, corporate and government solutions, business books, and research. AMA's approach to improving performance combines experiential learning—learning through doing—with opportunities for ongoing professional growth at every step of one's career journey.

Printing number
10 9 8 7 6 5 4 3 2 1

Dedicated to
Warren Bennis and Samuel Culbert

CONTENTS

FOREWORD

In today's world, your personal and professional survival depend on building "lifeline" relationships. Going it alone doesn't work. You need to create a dream team of people who will commit to your goals and support you at every step.

This isn't something you can achieve by manipulating people. In fact, in an age of social networking, the negative influence generated by insincere tactics and trickery can destroy your relationships and reputation in a heartbeat.

Real influence doesn't work that way. It grows over time, and it pulls more and more people into your orbit. That's because real influence isn't just about getting what you want. It's also about making sure the people who matter to you get what *they* want.

When you practice real influence, it doesn't matter if you start without money, power, or connections. The people Mark and John talk about in these pages often began with little in the bank. One or two had just arrived in the country, knowing absolutely no one. Yet in just a few years, they became "power influencers."

In this book, John and Mark will show you exactly how to do what they did. And they'll tell you how to do it in ways that make it easy to face yourself in the mirror.

When it comes to real influence, I can't think of any better mentors than these two remarkable people. John is an extraordinary executive coach whose clients include Apple, Cisco Systems, Disney, Nike, Raytheon, Frito-Lay, Merrill Lynch, Johnson & Johnson, NASA, St. Jude Children's Research Hospital, Genentech, and Yamaha—and his lectures at the UCLA Anderson School of Management are standing room only. And Mark, in addition to being a clinical psychiatrist and author of the best-selling book, *Just Listen*, is one of the world's most sought-after executive coaches, with a client list that includes GE, IBM, Merrill Lynch, Xerox, Deutsche Bank, Hyatt, Accenture, AstraZeneca, British Airways, ESPN, Federal Express, and the FBI. He's also one of the thought leaders at Ferrazzi Greenlight.

Don't let Mark and John fool you with their self-deprecating stories. They've both earned their worldwide influence by practicing the generosity, transparency, and honesty that shine through in these pages. As a result, they have an enormous tribe of friends and colleagues that spans countries and continents. I consider myself very lucky to be a member of it.

And you, in turn, are very lucky to be holding this book in your hands. That's because when you put the Connected Influence model into action, it will magnify your results, exponentially enhance your reputation, and empower you to create your own dream team of supporters. And more than that—it will change every relationship in your life for the better.

That's the power of real influence—and as Mark and John will show you, it's within your reach.

Keith Ferrazzi

Real Influence

INTRODUCTION

Are you frustrated because you fail to get people to buy into your great ideas, can't close the deal on tough sales, or constantly hit the wall when you try to influence people?

If so, you're not alone. As executive coaches, we know that it's harder than ever to influence people because *the old rules of persuasion no longer work.*

Today, we live in a postselling and postpushing world. As people grow more aware of manipulative tactics, their guard goes up. The Internet, television advertising, and wall-to-wall marketing have made us cynical about deceptive tricks and hard-sell approaches. Your customers, your coworkers, and even your kids can all recognize "pushy" influence . . . and when you use it, they'll push back twice as hard.

Yet most of the books and business school courses that teach persuasion skills emphasize manipulative tactics and techniques. They conceive of influence as something that you "do" to someone else to get your way. And they focus on short-term gains rather than long-term consequences.

We call this outdated strategy *disconnected* influence. It's a short-sighted strategy that sometimes creates momentary "buy-in" but often at the expense of your relationships and reputation. And it keeps you from making the deep, transformational connections that lead to great outcomes in your career and in your life.

To influence people in powerful ways that can change your future, you need to move from disconnected to *connected* influence. When you make this transition, you'll set the stage for strong, sustained influence by becoming the kind of person other people are eager to follow. These people won't just agree to support you. They'll line up to champion your causes, and they'll have your back whenever you need their help.

In this book, we've distilled the elements of connected influence into a simple four-step model for becoming wildly successful by being both influential and "influenceable." We've helped thousands of people master these four steps—and in the process, we've empowered them to save their companies, increase their sales, achieve business goals they thought were impossible, and take their personal relationships to an entirely new level.

But this book isn't just about our own experiences. In addition, we've interviewed more than one hundred remarkable influencers who are putting these same steps into action in their own lives. These people are using their powers of persuasion to change the world every day. They head international corporations, raise millions for charities, help kids with cancer, and work to save the planet. They personify success, and their stories illustrate the astonishing power of connected influence.

As you read these stories, here is what we want you to remember: No matter who you are and where you are in life, you can do what these people have done. In fact, the most powerful lesson the stories in this book illustrate is that *anyone can positively influence anyone else,* regardless of their differences in experience, status, age, income, or power. The people we talked with didn't start out with powerful connections, but they knew how to earn these connections and how to solidify and expand them. Their message is that there is no need—ever—to set limits in your influence potential. When you master the steps we outline in this book, you can influence anyone, even someone who "has it all."

This book won't tell you what you can accomplish by tricking people, manipulating them, or stepping on them. Instead, it will teach you how to be the kind of influencer that you and the people in your life want you to be. That's because as you build deeper relationships, you'll drive stronger results. And when you approach relationships by thinking about giving rather than getting, and about adding value before seeking value, you'll be amazed at the return you see on your investment.

When you put the ideas in this book to work in your own life, you'll learn what all the masters of influence in this book know. Connected influence pays off—and it pays forward. Connected influence multiplies, and as it multiplies, it leads to amazing outcomes.

Here's to yours.

SECTION 1

The Problem: Why Are You Struggling to Influence People?

You can use tricks and manipulation to gain short-term compliance, but disconnected influence doesn't earn you the commitment you need to achieve great things. Why? Because when you're stuck in **your here**, you can't get to **their there**—and that's where you need to be in order to persuade people effectively. In Section One, you'll discover the risks of disconnected influence and the four traps that cause you to fall into it. Then we'll share the secret for becoming a powerful influencer: the four simple steps of connected influence.

1

The Dangers
of "Disconnect"

You cannot antagonize and influence
at the same time.

J. S. Knox, in *Fundamentals of Success*

Did you ever try to get other people to do something that would be better for them, better for you, better for a project team or a company, better for their family or yours, or even better for the world . . . and fail?

Odds are you had good intentions. You had hard facts to support your point of view. Maybe you even set deadlines, offered rewards, or threatened penalties.

You tried your best, but they didn't budge.

It's an unhappy experience. But what's far worse is when it happens over and over again. And for millions of smart, caring, and creative people just like you, it does. Even when these people are right—when they have brilliant ideas, inspiring goals, or the best of intentions—they can't get through.

If they're managers, they can't light a spark under their teams. If they're in sales, they can't make the big plays. If they're in relationships, they can't get their partners or children to agree to their ideas. And if they have revolutionary ideas that could make the world better, they can't get anyone to listen.

This book is for them.

If you're one of these people, the methods you're using to influence people aren't working. They're not inspired by your vision, and they're not willing to share your goals. And here's why: *Most people, most of the time, aren't motivated to do what you want them to do.* They don't feel your urgency, they're busy with their own priorities and crises, or they have hidden reasons for rejecting your ideas.

To break down these walls, you need to create powerful connections that make people *want* to do what you're recommending. But you don't, because here's what you're thinking:

"How can I get my boss to . . . "
"How can I get my team to . . . "
"How can I get this client to . . . "
"How can I get my partner to . . . "
"How can I get my kids to . . . "
"How can I get this interviewer to . . . "

These are examples of disconnected influence. And they don't work.

On the surface, of course, disconnected influence makes perfect sense. You've got to get things done. Important priorities are at stake. You size up a situation and see gaps that need to be filled and mistakes that need to be fixed. Maybe your project team is making a foolish decision. Or your boss needs to allocate more money to your project. Or your daughter is dating someone who isn't good for her. Or your partner isn't sticking to your family budget.

But when you view influence as "getting people to do what I want," you actually *reduce* your influence. That's because you're viewing the person you're trying to influence as a target, an object, something to be pushed or pulled. You're not hearing the other person's message. And the other person either recognizes this immediately or—even if you get temporary compliance— resents it later.

Disconnected influence is what many business schools teach. It's what most experts teach. But if you have big goals and need long-term commitments, it's a prescription for failure.

To explain why, we'd like to start with a story. But be forewarned: The take-away lesson may surprise you.

> Scott is a manager at a large global healthcare firm. He's at a strategic off-site meeting today.
>
> Scott has a strong working relationship with Marcus, the vice president in charge of his division. Marcus values Scott's intellect, business acumen, and no-nonsense directness. He considers Scott the "honest broker" in the group—the person Marcus can count on to speak the truth even when it's risky.
>
> In today's meeting, an important issue involving new hires comes up. Marcus makes a quick decision and tells the group to move on to the next issue.
>
> Scott speaks up: "Wait a minute. Can we take a look at this decision? There are a lot of implications here."
>
> "No," says Marcus, "we're moving on."
>
> Scott knows Marcus is making a mistake. The distribution of new hires will have a huge impact on how well Marcus's team performs. There are crucial questions to ask and trade-offs to consider. Scott and Marcus have been discussing an exciting new project for the team, and this decision could make it much harder to launch.
>
> Scott chooses his next words carefully. "But Marcus," he says calmly and respectfully, "let's consider a couple of things that I expect everyone will agree are important to discuss for the good of the organization as a whole."

Marcus says firmly, "Scott, I've made my decision."

Scott is confused, but he knows he's right. He's not trying to pick a fight. He's not trying to score points. He's simply hoping to stop Marcus from making a decision that could harm the whole team. No one else will speak up, and he knows Marcus will appreciate his honesty later. It's up to him.

So he says, "I understand, but I think it would help to . . . "

Marcus cuts him off sharply, "*Enough*. We're moving on. The next issue is . . . "

Scott is stunned. He feels devalued and disrespected. He's only trying to do the right thing, and he has the knowledge and expertise to back up his concerns. He's frustrated, and he leans back and folds his arms. He's angry that Marcus is behaving in an authoritarian manner, making abrupt choices on a complex issue, and cutting him off rudely. Scott won't act out, but he's displeased, and they're going to talk about it later.

This is an unpleasant situation, and it's likely to get worse. It's the kind of disagreement that can cause a close-knit team to fracture, or even make a top performer like Scott think about leaving.

But here's the thing.

It's not Marcus who's screwing up.

It's Scott.

■ The "Blind Spot" in Our Brains

Why are we pointing the finger at Scott, who is the rational, respectful manager who's trying to make a logical point while his boss is riding roughshod over him?

Because Scott is making a dangerous mistake. He's practicing disconnected influence—"How can I get Marcus to do what I want?" He's completely focused on his own point of view, and as a result, he's failing to connect with Marcus. And that means he's operating in his blind spot.

To get a feel for this, imagine you're driving on the highway. You scan everything around you through the windshield and the rearview and sideview mirrors. The road is clear, so you move into the next lane.

The next instant, you feel a thud and hear a wrenching of metal. Your heart leaps into your throat as you realize you've sideswiped a motorcyclist who was coming up behind you. From your perspective, he "came out of nowhere." But he was there all along. You just didn't see him, because you didn't check your blind spot.

What does this have to do with influence? Your brain doesn't merely have a blind spot when it comes to driving; it also has a blind spot when it comes to *influencing*. And like a driver who changes lanes without checking to see what's in the blind spot, you're dangerous when you're blinded by your own point of view.

When you practice disconnected influence, you're stuck in what we call **your here**. You can see *your* position, *your* facts, and *your* intentions clearly. But to connect with the people you're trying to influence, you need to communicate from a perspective we call **their there**. You need to see *their* position, *their* facts, and *their* intentions clearly. And you can't reach **their there** if you can't see it. From your point of view, these people are invisible—just like the motorcyclist.

And that brings us back to Scott. Because he's focused solely on his own message, he's communicating from his **here**. As a result, his brain has a blind spot when it comes to Marcus's **there**—and that's where he gets into trouble.

Scott and Marcus do talk later, but things don't go the way Scott expects them to. Scott is expecting an apology from Marcus. Instead, Marcus shuts the door and says tersely, "Sit down." Then he lights into Scott.

"You ignored the clear signals I sent you," Marcus says. "You know I respect your opinions. You know I don't normally cut you off. You know I don t make snap decisions. So you should have realized that I did what I did for a reason."

As it turned out, upper management was planning a reorganization that would affect Scott's peers and their teams. Things weren't entirely settled, and the senior team needed to keep the discussions confidential until the final decisions were made. Marcus knew that discussing the new hires would quickly put him into an ethical bind, because he'd have to say things that weren't true.

"I was annoyed when you continued to press the matter," Marcus says, "but I know that's what you do—and usually I appreciate it. But what really disappointed me is how you sulked afterwards and tuned me out. That was immature."

Three months later, on Scott's next performance review, along with the usual excellent ratings and comments, there's a critical entry for the very first time: "However, sometimes when Scott doesn't get his way, he's prone to act with immaturity and petulance."

Scott made a huge mistake in the meeting because he was blind to the urgent messages Marcus was sending him. He was so sure he was right that the only question he asked himself was, "How do I stop Marcus from doing this?" He completely missed the real question: "Why is Marcus doing this?" As a result, he jeopardized a great outcome—the innovative project he and Marcus were envisioning for their team—by creating a rift that may be permanent.

This kind of error isn't rare. In fact, it's nearly universal when you approach situations from *your here*. It's virtually a given that there's some important clue you're missing—and that clue is keeping you from influencing another person.

And here's another important point: You're most likely to make this mistake when you have the best of intentions. Notice that Scott didn't screw up because he was self-serving or because he ignored what was best for his team. In fact, it took a lot of courage for him to keep challenging Marcus. But he did it because he knew he was right.

And that's the irony: Good intentions can steer good people the wrong way. In effect, they expand our blind spot. When you feel committed to doing the right thing, you can easily give yourself too much benefit of the doubt and ignore what other people are trying to tell you. Worse yet, a belief in your own rightness can encourage you to fall back on tactics, tricks, and maneuvers to gain short-term compliance

Put another way, good intentions often create a sort of intellectual and emotional laziness. We use our high-mindedness to justify failing to take the time to get where other people are coming from and why. Sure that what we want is best, we keep driving forward under the blinding confidence of our good intentions. We're convinced that we don't need to learn or hear more from others, that other options and alternatives don't exist, that our agenda is the single best plan possible, and that we're justified in using any means to achieve it. And we're nearly always wrong.

And what if we *aren't* wrong? It doesn't matter. We still lose.

That's because even if what we want is best for all concerned, other people don't want it shoved down their throats. They want to align with us, work with us, and be valued by us. They don't want to be run over by us. If we trample them to get our way, we may get them to do what we want right now, but they'll be angry about it later . . . and they'll let other people know.

People tell us they often sense the vibe changing when someone moves from apparent listening to clumsy influencing. They feel baited into lowering their guards, and then they switch into a defensive posture as the self-interested agenda becomes evident. ("Hey Joe, it's great to talk with you after all these years. We had some great times back then, didn't we? Anyway, I see you're doing well in your job, and what a coincidence, because I was looking to get hired at your company . . . ")

Even if your approach is subtler, people will sense it: "Okay, here's where you go from caring about me to all about you. Next, you're going to push me to do something I don't want to do." It's dispiriting for them to realize that in your universe, they're not people but merely props.

And here's the biggest problem of all with the manipulative influence techniques many experts recommend—techniques often based on social science experiments. These experiments typically stop measuring after people comply, as if no aftereffects come into play. But real life consists of a web of relationships and reputations that spread far beyond an initial interchange. In the real world, interactions are never isolated. Anything you do might affect your relationships, as well as your reputation, for a long time to come.

▪ The Solution: See Past Your Blind Spot

In a busy world where you're competing for people's attention, it's perfectly fine to use a few tricks to get people to listen to you. But once they're listening, you can't cheat them. If they sense that you're focused entirely on your own viewpoint and can't see theirs, they'll cooperate just as far as they need to—and no further. And the next time you need them, they won't be there.

To reach these people and win their long-term support, you

need to stop pushing. You need to stop "selling." You need to stop focusing on what you want them to do. And you need to stop using sleight-of-hand schemes to trick them.

Instead, you need to influence them in ways that spark a genuine connection. You need to see their vision and make it part of yours. You need to make them want to work with you to achieve amazing outcomes . . . and that means you need to start from ***their there***. It's the secret for building long-term commitments—and for reaching big goals. Here's an example.

Giselle Chapman wanted to work as a pharmaceutical sales rep, but she got turned down at every interview.

Giselle asked why she wasn't getting the job. Each time, she got the same answer: The managers wanted people with at least two years of experience in the pharmaceutical industry.

So she asked a follow-up question: Why is two years of experience important?

Her interviewers answered: "Because experienced pharmaceutical reps have a much better chance of getting in to see physicians. Those are our key customers. It takes time to understand the environment in medical offices, know how to navigate conversations and build relationships with influencers, and ultimately get in to see the doctors."

Giselle said, "Thank you."

A couple of days later, she went to a medical building and took the elevator to the top floor. She started there and worked her way down, going into each office on each floor and asking, "May I please speak with the person who normally sees pharmaceutical sales reps?" In many cases they said yes, and in several of those cases the person was a physician. To those doctors she said, "I'm doing interviews to find out what's going well and what should be different, to help improve the service you get."

Toward the end of her next job interview, Giselle asked, "Is there any reason I wouldn't be the candidate of choice?" Once again, the hiring manager said that she lacked experience.

Giselle asked, "If you knew that I could get in to see physicians, are you confident enough in your training program that I could do well in this industry?"

The hiring manager said "absolutely"—they had one of the best training programs in the industry.

Giselle said, "Last week I saw ten of your customers. Would you like to hear what I learned?"

"What?!"

Giselle said, "I met with physicians from ten different medical groups last week. I gathered data on what they need that they're not getting from their pharmaceutical companies. Would that be of interest to you?"

The hiring manager said, "You have no company, no business card, and you got in to see physicians? If you did that, don't move. I can get you hired before you go to a competitor for your next interview."

Giselle Chapman was hired by Bristol-Myers Squibb, one of the leading pharmaceutical companies at that time. She became their number one sales representative, and went on to form her own consulting company.

Giselle won her first pharmaceutical industry job by doing what almost no job candidate does: She visualized a great outcome both for her and for her interviewer. She went from her **here** (I'm smart, I'm a go-getter, I want this job) to her interviewer's **there** (we need someone who can get in to see physicians and learn what they want). When she did this, she engaged the interviewer's attention, offered something of value, and—in the end—got the job she wanted.

Now, we're not saying that connected influence like this is effortless. In fact, we're going to tell you right now that it takes hard work to do what Giselle did. It means going beyond "What works for me?" and thinking, "What works for everyone?" And it means focusing on long-term benefits rather than quick victories.

If you're up for this challenge, we'll show you how to use the same approaches Giselle used to succeed in a job interview, inspire your team or your family, or sell a great idea. When you follow the steps we lay out, you'll move from disconnected to connected influence . . . and like the power influencers we interviewed, you'll transform your relationships and even your life.

In the following pages, you'll see how the people we interviewed used connected influence to achieve everything from convincing Ray Charles to make his amazing last recording to saving Nike from a multimillion-dollar mistake. But first, there's one more thing we need to talk about. To become highly influential, you're going to need to break some bad habits. And that means you need to be aware of four traps of human nature that are stopping you from succeeding right now.

2

Four Traps That
"Disconnect" You

Things do not change;
we change.
Henry David Thoreau

When you practice connected influence, an entirely new level of opportunity arises. It's not just about getting people to do what you want right now. It's about getting long-term buy-in from everyone: your team, your business unit, your organization, your clients, your family.

But before you can reach this goal, you need to understand where you're starting out. And that means recognizing that you have some serious baggage.

As you master the elements of the connected influence model, you're going to start freeing yourself from four "bad influence" habits that keep you disconnected. We call them *human nature traps*, and you can't fully overcome them because they're hardwired into your brain—but you can avoid them more successfully when you can spot yourself falling into them. Here's a look at all four, and why they're so dangerous.

■ The Fight or Flight Response

The first trap that leads you to disconnect may sound a little crazy. But here it is: You're an animal.

To put it more accurately, you're only partly human—especially when you're stressed. If you've read Mark's book, *Just Listen*, you already know what we're talking about here. But even if this isn't news to you, stay with us, because we'd like you to think about it from a different angle.

Here's the short story: In effect, you have not one brain but three. That's because Mother Nature has spent hundreds of thousands of years fine-tuning your brain's hardware and software. But she didn't get rid of the old parts; instead, she just added on to them.

As a result, you have three different "layers" of brains, and each one has a purpose. Your reptile brain focuses on *fight or flight*, your mammalian brain on *emotion*, and your human brain on *reason*.

This is actually a very efficient system most of the time, because each of these parts knows its job. Your human brain is at work when you're entering data in a spreadsheet, your mammal brain feels happy when you're holding a baby, and your reptile brain screams "Run!" if a car swerves toward you.

The problem is that sometimes your three brains can get in the way of each other—especially when you're under stress.

At times like this, an emotional sensor in your brain called the amygdala can become overly activated, causing what psychologist Daniel Goleman calls "amygdala hijack." When your amygdala gets hijacked, it's as if your three brains have disconnected and are all functioning independently of each other. At this point, think of yourself as human, mammal, and reptile . . . and the human is only partly in charge.

And it gets worse. As your agitation escalates, the 245-million-year-old "fight or flight" reptilian part of your brain takes increasing control. This means you can't assess the situation based on what's happening in the present. Instead, your amygdala throws you into reacting based on an old, hardwired response. Your thinking gets distorted, your emotions run high, and your behaviors become primitive.

This quickly creates a vicious cycle, because the more snakelike you get, the more agitated your amygdala becomes. Pretty soon, your human and mammal brains are entirely out of the loop. So you're not connecting with people logically, and you're not connecting with them emotionally. Instead, you're cornered in **your here**, and you want to either escape from the people who are upsetting you or hurt them.

Of course, today's meeting rooms and phone conferences are far away in space and time from the prehistoric predator vs. prey conditions under which the brain developed these responses. But your nervous system doesn't care. It doesn't know the difference between a tyrannosaurus and a tyrannical boss. So while amygdala hijack probably won't make you run out of the room shrieking or hit someone over the head with a stick, it can definitely cause you to "lose it" on a purely biological level.

When that happens, you'll typically go for one of two fundamental strategies. Unfortunately, both are deeply flawed.

The first is flight—"go away." This is about avoidance and inaction. It's an absence of influence. It's disengaging or freezing up when it would serve you better to take action. It's capitulating, giving in, or avoiding the choice, the risk, or the opportunity.

The second is fight—"go push." Here's where you try to nudge, cajole, convince, or force your counterpart into compliance.

The four mistakes you frequently commit in the PUSH state are:

P = Pressing your case too much instead of striving to understand your counterpart's point of view.

U = Understating alternatives in favor of your preset agenda.

S = Short-term focusing by going for quick self-serving advantage rather than setting the stage for sustained success by building relationships and enhancing your reputation.

H = Hassling by turning every discussion into a fight, which tells people that it's more about your ego than about a commitment to shared goals.

When you're in snake mode, you're not going to influence anyone, so it's important to avoid this trap. The best strategy for preventing amygdala hijack is to get out of **your here.** That's because when you're focused on your own fears, your own stress, and your own anger, you're continually re-agitating your amygdala. Once you focus on what other people are feeling, you turn the heat in your own mind down to a simmer . . . and you can engage instead of escaping or attacking.

Although he frequently appears on television and radio, Mark is shy by nature. In fact, years ago, he was so shy that at parties he'd hang out by the onion dip staring at his watch for a couple of hours and then beg his wife to leave.

It wasn't working for him, and it definitely wasn't working for her. So one evening Mark tried something different. He decided that he'd speak to three people at the party, focusing on making *them* happy that he'd talked with them.

Mark didn't know what was going to happen. But by the end of the evening, he'd enjoyed terrific conversations with five people. Three of them even took his hand with both hands, smiled at him, and told him how much they enjoyed meeting him and wanted to follow up with him.

When Mark left the party—and this time he stayed so long that his wife was begging *him* to leave—he wondered why his crippling shyness had disappeared during his conversations. Then he realized that instead of dwelling on the **his here** of his own discomfort and nervousness and going into amygdala hijack, he went to **their there** by "just listening" and focusing on being more interested than interesting. When he did that, he found a place where his mind felt safe.

▪ The Habit Handicap

The second human nature trap is one we're vulnerable to when we're deeply stressed. In this situation, it's difficult to generate new ideas and find different ways of thinking, feeling, and acting. That's because under pressure, we typically do one of two things: We go into amygdala hijack, or we go to our comfort zone. In the second scenario—habit handicap—we do what we're used to doing. We do what usually works. For instance:

- People who steer toward logic and analysis may repeat the same argument over and over, or talk in a louder or slower voice. They may even keep saying, "You don't understand . . . " or "You're not getting it" or "You're not listening."
- Peacemakers may placate people by giving in to anything they want.

Whatever pattern we fall into, we go there because that's where we're on familiar ground. It's our port in a storm.

The problem is that our old patterns rarely fit our current circumstances. That's why we feel especially challenged and frustrated when we're trying to influence people in high-pressure business situations. It's not really about what's happening to us at that moment. It's about a behavioral reflex that's getting in the way of analyzing the situation we're in.

As comedian Adam Carolla says, "If you put a beaver on the top floor of the Empire State building, it will start looking around for wood to build a dam." It's the same with us: Ingrained habit combined with the stress response of our neural system puts us at the mercy of our own dysfunctional default settings. We're stuck in a pattern of ineffective behavior. We're stuck at **our here**. Here's an example.

> Sharon was an engineer in a large aerospace company. She had a master's degree from MIT and a solid track record of success built by working with teams tasked to some of the most challenging technical problems.
>
> By nature she was focused, determined, and competitive. Outside of work, she was a successful triathlete. At work, she stood out as an extremely insightful and valuable team member, and even won two top awards given annually by senior leadership to recognize individuals for engineering excellence.
>
> On task teams assigned to tough technical challenges, Sharon shined. Her normal style served her and her teammates well. She was direct and blunt. She could quickly find holes in the thinking of others and routinely said things like:
>
> "Here's where you're wrong . . . "
> "You didn't think about . . . "
> "That's not right . . . "
> "That won't work . . . "
> "You should have done this instead . . . "
>
> Sharon's teams thrived in a Darwinian marketplace of contributions, where the best ideas survived and ineffective ideas died unceremoniously. Participants engaged in vigorous debate and conflict around task solutions. It worked for them because they focused on results and tended not to take things personally.

After a few years, Sharon was rewarded for her success with a promotion to senior director. Her new role involved significant levels of coordination across different functions in the organization. Instead of dealing primarily with fellow engineers, she now dealt with nonengineer managers who tackled very different types of problems and were used to interacting in much more collaborative ways.

To these leaders, Sharon's brusque style of pointing out what she saw as their faults and errors came across as insulting and ill informed. The "here's where you're wrong" type of statements that the engineers accepted calmly raised the hackles of managers who thought she was rude and abrasive.

Instead of assessing her style and considering whether it worked in her new environment, Sharon tried to strengthen her approach. This was her version of the habit handicap. She wasn't having her typical impact, so she reasoned that she needed to present her views even more forcefully. As a result, she alienated people to an even greater degree, and they started shutting her out of the decision-making process.

As Sharon's example shows, habit handicap can make you respond to failure by doubling down. When things aren't working, the *your here* perspective encourages you to think, "They missed it; they're not getting it." It's easy to conclude you need to do it again, perhaps with even more intensity. However, as Albert Einstein said, the definition of insanity is "doing the same thing over and over again and expecting different results."

By contrast, going to *their there* encourages you to ask questions: Why are they responding the way they are? How is my behavior contributing to that? What can I do instead? It breaks the habit handicap and allows you to see the present situation instead of refighting the last war.

■ Error Blindness: It Feels So Right to Be Wrong

The third human nature trap that can keep you in the blind spot of *your here* has to do with making mistakes. And here, we're talking about a special category of mistakes—the ones you don't yet know that you've made.

We talked in Chapter One about how the "get them to do what I want" mind-set puts you at high risk for missing vital information or even being completely wrong about an issue or a person. It's hard to realize that you might be wrong when you think you're right—especially when your logic, analysis, emotions, experience, and preparation all point toward your conclusion. As Mark Twain said, "It ain't what you don't know that gets you into trouble. It's what you know for sure that just ain't so."

One of the best descriptions we've ever heard of error blindness is Kathryn Schulz's TED.com talk, "On Being Wrong." In her presentation, Schulz, a self-described "wrongologist," asks a provocative question: How does it feel to be wrong?

From the audience she gets answers such as "dreadful" and "embarrassing." But she explains that these are answers to a different question: "How does it feel to *realize* you're wrong?" Realizing you're wrong can feel dreadful and embarrassing, or it can be devastating, or revelatory, or even funny.

But just *being* wrong, she says, doesn't feel like anything. She draws an analogy to the cartoon coyote who speedily chases a roadrunner until his momentum carries him over a cliff. The roadrunner is fine; being a bird, it simply flies away. But after the coyote goes over the edge, he hangs suspended in the air for a few moments. He can't fly, and running isn't working anymore. He hovers, temporarily defying gravity. In the cartoon, it's only when he looks down and realizes there's no ground beneath him that he falls.

Schulz makes the point that *while* we're being wrong, we're like the coyote in midair before he looks down. We think we're okay, even though what we're doing isn't working, because we don't know it yet. In other words, being wrong feels like being right. We get stuck inside a state she calls "error blindness."

While we're in that midair state of misguidedly confident error blindness, we're tempted to make a sequence of assumptions about our counterparts. Schulz describes how we tend to escalate our negative attributions when people stubbornly refuse to agree with us by going through the following three stages:

The ignorance assumption: They don't know and it needs to be explained to them.

The idiocy assumption: They're not smart enough, and it needs to be explained again.

The evil assumption: They're working against us.

Each of these assumptions keeps you locked into **your here**, and prevents you from going to **their there**. Still worse, the disrespectful actions and the resentful attitude you take based on these assumptions can damage your relationships and reputation.

A while ago, John was teaching a leadership course for visiting international students at the UCLA Anderson School of Management. On the first day of class, the doors were locked and the students were left standing in the hall. The course met in a room that wasn't used very often, so it was understandable. John went down one floor to the facilities manager and asked him to open the classroom.

On the second day of class, the students were locked out again. John asked for help and clarified the schedule with the facilities manager to make sure the doors would be unlocked the next time.

On the third day when John approached the room, he saw the students once again standing around outside. He shook his head and went straight to the facilities manager. With clear annoyance in his voice (which pains him to recall), he asked the facilities manager to please open the door *and* ensure that the door was open every day at the right time so these international visitors wouldn't be wasting their time and feeling ill treated.

The facilities manager looked surprised. "It's not open?" he asked.

John said sharply, "No. It's not," while thinking to himself, "Sheesh . . . would I be here if it were open?"

"Hmmm, I'm surprised," said the facilities manager. "Of course, let me go up and unlock it. I'm sorry about that."

At this point, John was the coyote over the cliff, full of confidence but not yet looking down.

He and the facilities manager went up to the room together. The facilities manager pulled on the door handle, and it opened. No key required.

It turned out that a few students were seated in the room. But the majority of them were enjoying hanging out in the hallway. They were relaxing, drinking their coffee, and conversing before going into the room and taking their seats. They were just waiting for John to arrive.

Because the door was locked the first two times, John assumed it was locked a third time. He also assumed the students were annoyed. Confident in his assumptions, he hadn't even bothered checking the door.

John felt foolish. He hadn't understood why his students were gathering in the hall, he'd falsely implied that the facility manager was incompetent, and he'd wasted everyone's time by having the facilities manager come back up to the classroom.

He'd had multiple opportunities to go to **their there** in this situation, and he'd missed them all. He could have tried to open the door to the room, asked the students why they were in the hall, or spoken at more length (and in a more understanding way) with the facilities manager. But he was too stuck in error blindness to even consider any of these options.

Embarrassed, John apologized to the facilities manager for not checking the door and for his curt tone.

"No problem," said the facilities manager, "mistakes happen. Part of the job." The man smiled, shook John's hand, and taught him yet another lesson in how to be more gracious even when you think you're right.

■ The Double Curse of Knowledge

The error blindness trap ensnares us when we're wrong, but our fourth human nature trap catches us when we're right. That's because being right also has its own dangers and shortcomings.

Most of the time, our knowledge and experience serve us well. But when we run into influence challenges—when we're failing to persuade and finding it difficult to get things done with people—what we "know" can change from asset to obstacle.

Why? Because it's very difficult to "unknow" what you know. And this can create enormous gaps between **your here** and **their there**.

In their wonderful book, *Made to Stick*, Chip and Dan Heath describe Elizabeth Newton's thought-provoking research about gaps in communication. Newton performed a now-famous experiment in which she divided a group of people into two roles: "tappers" and "listeners." The tappers chose from a list of well-known songs such as *Happy Birthday to You* and *The Star Spangled Banner*. Then they tapped the rhythms of their songs on a table for their designated listeners, who were asked to guess the song.

Before starting, the tappers predicted that listeners would guess the song correctly 50 percent of the time. It turned out that listeners only guessed 2.5 percent of the songs correctly. Instead of one out of two correct guesses, it turned out to be one out of forty. That's a big difference.

Why? Because the tappers were stuck in **your here**. They heard the song in their head while they were tapping. It's impossible *not* to hear the song while you're tapping. But the listeners were in **their there**. All they heard, as the Heaths put it, were "a bunch of disconnected taps, like a kind of bizarre Morse code."

Even more revealing when it comes to interpersonal influence is how the tappers reacted to the listeners. They were flustered, frustrated, and flabbergasted. They couldn't believe the listeners weren't getting it. The facial expressions and body language of the tappers showed their dismay at the listeners' apparent intellectual deficiency. (Remember Kathryn Schulz's ignorance assumption and idiocy assumption?) They thought, "Something is wrong with the listeners! How could they be so dumb?"

But there was nothing wrong with the listeners. They just had a different perspective.

The Heaths call what the tappers experienced "the curse of knowledge." The tappers couldn't "un-hear" the tune in their head while they were tapping, which made it very difficult for them to empathize with the listeners. They were "cursed" with the knowledge of what the song was and how it sounded. They had a blind spot in their brain about what it was like to *not* hear that song while it was being tapped. It was much easier to think there was something wrong with the listeners than to make the difficult mental and emotional journey from **your here** to **their there**.

In the tapping experiment, there was nothing important at stake—yet the gap between **your here** and **their there** led participants to experience frustration and annoyance. Needless to say, the results can be far more damaging when you're trying to get things done with people in the real world.

> Some years ago John was working with a business team headed by Lucas, a vice president in a telecommunications firm. During a discussion about priorities, Lucas broke in to say, "As everyone knows, there are five things we need to accomplish within the next year. If we don't, all these other topics we're talking about are irrelevant."
>
> As John looked around the room, it was clear from the expressions on people's faces that they didn't know what Lucas thought everyone knew. But no one felt comfortable enough to ask Lucas to clarify what he meant, and he didn't notice.
>
> Lucas didn't realize that he was a tapper and the others were confused listeners. He was sure everyone was at **his here**, and couldn't imagine there was any **their there** that was relevant. As a result, his audience was frustrated, and no one was sure where the discussion was heading.
>
> John asked Lucas if he would list the five items, but Lucas said it was a waste of time to do so. He knew the issues, and everyone around the table knew the issues.
>
> During a break, John pulled Lucas aside and convinced him to write down the items in a numbered list on a flipchart. If everyone on the team could see the items, John pointed out, they'd all be on the same page and they could refer to the items by number. Even if everyone knew all the items, it would help to avoid confusion.

Lucas agreed and started writing. The end of the break came, but Lucas was still writing, so John extended the break. When the group at last reconvened, Lucas had his list. But the expected five items had turned out to be eight items, which raised even more questions. This led to a very productive discussion in which the team, for the first time, *truly* got aligned about their priorities.

Lucas turned out to be a tapper suffering from the curse of knowledge when it came to assuming that his team knew which five items he was talking about. And he was simultaneously suffering from a case of error blindness when he forgot the other three items himself. As a result, he'd nearly sabotaged an important meeting in which matters crucial to his company's future were at stake.

One reason the divide between tappers and listeners is so much more dangerous in real life is that the curse of knowledge becomes the "double curse" of knowledge. In the real world, it isn't just about them not getting you. It's also about you not getting them.

That's why the people who are most successful at exercising positive influence over time don't think and act like tappers trying to get listeners in line. The best influencers realize they're both tappers and listeners themselves, with an emphasis on being the listener because that's the harder part.

The best influencers also understand that the double curse of knowledge is in play in *all* of their interactions. These people realize that it's all too easy to overestimate their own clarity when they're communicating, and they're aware that they're not always getting the full message when other people are trying to get through. It's this knowledge that saves them from appearing arrogant and condescending when people "just don't get it."

▪ Avoid Hardwired Traps by Rewriting Your Software

The human nature traps we've talked about are all the more challenging because they're not our fault—we're hardwired to fall into them. Our three-part brain leaves us vulnerable to amygdala hijack. We're biologically wired to see things from our own perspective. And our brains aren't anywhere near as rational as we like to think.

That's why you can sometimes fall into these traps even when you know they exist. But you'll do it far less when you discover how to go beyond the limitations of your brain's hardware by writing new software that lets you move from *your here* to *their there* in every important relationship. When you do this, you can create new habits that set the stage for you to have more genuine, lasting influence with other people. And that's what the connected influence model is all about.

3

The Four Steps to Connecting and Influencing

Leadership is having people follow
you not because they have to,
but because they want to.
Larry Wilson, organizational consultant

We recognize disconnected influence when we encounter it. It's the CEO who wins by bullying, the manager who's trapped in error blindness, the salesperson who tricks us into buying something we don't want, or the "friend" who manipulates our feelings. And we recognize the feelings these people create in us: anger, frustration, resentment, and disappointment.

But here's an interesting thing: We don't always notice connected influence when it's happening. That's because we don't feel like we're being pushed or tricked, misunderstood, ignored, or threatened. So we don't shove back. Instead, we willingly *lean into* the influence because we implicitly trust the person who's influencing us. This makes connected influence as powerful as it is subtle.

As we've spoken with the hundreds of powerful "influencers" we interviewed for this book, as well as thousands of participants at our workshops and conferences, one question we've asked is: "Who influences *you*?" And what we've discovered is that the people who are best at persuading aren't forceful persuaders.

Instead, the people who are most influential to us are inspirational. They serve as role models by setting an example we want to live up to. They see more in us than we see in ourselves. They inspire us to see beyond what we want to do and instead see what we could do. They call us toward possibility. They change us for the better. They do more than influence us. They help us be better persons. They help us be better bosses, colleagues, friends, spouses, siblings, and parents.

In addition, they're the people who stand up *for* us when we can't stand up for ourselves, stand *by* us and won't let us fail, and sometimes stand up *to* us when we're going astray. They're the people who have our backs . . . even before we have theirs. And as they willingly reach for **our here**, they draw us into **their there**.

When we ask people to describe the people they consider most influential in their lives, we hear comments like these over and over:

> "This person made me who I am today."
> "I'm so grateful to him."
> "I would do anything for her because she would do the same for me."
> "I was a nobody years ago, and he went out of his way to help me."
> "If she asks me for something, I say yes because I trust her."
> "His esteem for me is one of the most precious gifts I can receive."

These answers reveal the secret behind real influence: You don't achieve it simply by doing things that buy you short-term victories.

Instead, you need to become the kind of person others are eager to follow.

That's why the connected influence model isn't a collection of strategies for manipulating people. Instead, it's a new way of acting *every day*. And it won't just change your business relationships; it will change all of your relationships by allowing you to overcome your blind spots and human nature traps so you can connect with the people who matter to you.

Here are the core principles of the connected influence philosophy:

■ It's about building a network of people who want to hear you out, help and support you, rather than leaving behind a list of people who feel disconnected, transacted, used, maneuvered, or manipulated to serve your self-interest.

■ It's about making the journey from **your here** to **their there** so you can understand other people's point of view, learn from it, engage them based on it, and add to it.

■ It's about identifying outcomes worthy of the people you want to connect with.

■ It's about being open and transparent about what you're doing, rather than concealing tactics and techniques in the hope those hidden or secret sources of leverage will "work" on them.

■ It's about easing the ache inside skeptical and even cynical people so they can trust safely.

As you practice the steps of connected influence, you'll trade *instrumental* influence for *inspirational* influence. When you make this transition, you'll see power, influence, and relationships in an entirely new light:

Disconnected Influence *"Influence is about getting what I want"*	Connected Influence *"Influence is about leading others to better results"*
Dividing other people into **adversaries and allies**	Viewing other people as **collaborators,** regardless of whether you disagree with them
Using techniques and tactics that generate **conditional compliance**	Striving to gain sustained commitment
Taking things **personally** when others object and resist	Understanding **why** others object and resist
Focusing on the short term so you can prevail on the issue at hand	**Viewing your current actions as a springboard** for future relationships, reputation, and results

When you incorporate the elements of connected influence into your life, you'll persuade without pushing. You'll succeed in highly competitive situations with difficult people who normally are not prone to collaborate. People will be less inclined to be suspicious or adversarial and more inclined to explore possibilities. And frequently, you'll make amazing things happen together.

> Giang Biscan, known as the "Start-Up Angel" in Los Angeles, is living proof that you can build influence even where relationships and resources don't yet exist. With little money or existing connections, she created a powerful network and reputation from scratch by adding value without waiting to be asked.
>
> When we asked her how she built her reputation, she said, "Not long ago, nobody knew me. But I'm truly passionate about what I do, and I'm not worried about what I will get back from others. I looked for business start-up events and offered to help. After a while, you help a number of people, and it spreads.

Sometimes at events I would just show up and take photos, and then send the photos to the meeting organizers and speakers. I'd carry my camera around, snapping all sorts of pictures, and they'd think I must be an official photographer. They liked the pictures, and that became a basis for conversation and a way to get to know each other."

At other events, Giang simply would arrive early to help set things up, finding that people often treated her as if she were part of the official event. That got her in communication with the event organizers and other key players, and she learned how to add more and more value, which in turn initiated more connections and relationships. She didn't "push" her way into these events and circles of influence. She "helped" her way in.

Giang read blogs and watched the news to see which speakers and events Los Angeles groups were hosting. Then she would go into action long in advance of the events, adding value without any expectations.

"There was one organization with a great reputation that holds large conferences," she said. "It costs six thousand dollars to attend, and the ratio of investors to entrepreneurs is more than two to one. The start-ups accepted into the event are rigorously screened, such that there is a seventy-five percent track record of start-ups being acquired at these events. I heard they were doing screening for Los Angeles, so on my own, I sent out invitations."

The organization noticed what she was doing and contacted her, asking "Who are you?" She got into the event for free, took photos and shared them, wrote about the event, and spread the word. Now they consult her every time they come to Los Angeles.

She also watches on Twitter for prominent investors who are coming from outside of Los Angeles, and then reaches out, asking, "Can I organize a small coffee with six start-ups in Los Angeles for you?" They say yes. Then she reaches out to start-ups and says, "Influential investors are coming to town, who wants to go?" For example, she saw that Don Dodge, who makes acquisitions for Google, tweeted a photo of the Santa Monica Pier. That meant he was in town. Immediately she put the word out and organized a meeting. Giang says, "I think about what both sides want and need, and I try to put the pieces together to make it easy for people to say yes."

In essence, Giang creates value out of thin air. She says, "That's the thesis of the whole business start-up community—it starts with ideas and passion." As a result, she now has start-ups and investors coming to her, offering equity and paying significant fees. And today, she's one of the most influential figures in the Los Angeles business start-up community.

Success stories like Giang's are within your reach, but they don't happen by magic. They require a willingness to take risks and an ability to set your own ego aside. And it's crucial to understand that you won't be out to win alone. You'll be out to help *everyone* win.

If this is a challenge that you're excited to take, you're ready to begin practicing connected influence. On page 39, see the four core steps to moving from **your here** to **their there** and becoming the powerful influencer you want to be.

■ Connected Influence in Action

In these pages, we've made a bold claim. We've told you that by practicing the connected influence method, it's possible to influence without compromising your values, to connect with people you thought were unreachable, to get results without trampling over

The Connected-Influence Model

Go for great outcomes.
This isn't just a once-a-year exercise in setting ambitious goals. It's about standing for something noble and worthwhile, and it's about going beyond where people want to be and showing them where they could be.

Listen past your blind spot.
To exert real influence, you need to have a willingness to learn, an open mind, and sometimes the insight to discover that you're wrong.

Engage them in *their there.*
Engaging strengthens the connection that comes from listening. It's about "getting" your audience—not using "gotcha" techniques to manipulate them into compliance.

When you've done enough . . . do more.
Doing more isn't just about the transactions you have with other people right now. It's about committing to making *their* great outcomes happen, both now and in the future, and leaving them awe-struck by your generosity.

others, and to achieve amazing outcomes. Now we want to show you how it's done in real life.

At the outset, however, we want to say that we understand if you're skeptical that the four simple steps we've outlined can create dramatic changes in your business relationships and your life. In your position, we'd be skeptical too. And that's why we're going to go away.

No, not entirely. But after this chapter, we're going to step back and let the influencers we've interviewed do most of the talking. In Sections Two to Five of this book, we'll explore one element of connected influence at a time and show how it works in the real world.

As our influencers relate their personal stories, we want you to discover just how powerful the elements of connected influence are when it comes to changing people, teams, companies, families, and even the world. We hope their experiences will inspire you to challenge your own perceived limits and begin to imagine just how far positive influence can take you.

SECTION 2

STEP #1
Go for Great Outcomes

To become a master at connected influence, you need to inspire people by going for what's possible—and then looking beyond that for what still *might* be possible. And remember that it's not the size of your goal that makes an outcome great. It's the ambition to make a difference, the courage to put yourself on the line for a principle, and the willingness to let everyone join in your success. Above all, as you'll see in this section, it's a determination to focus on the three "R"s of a great outcome: Results, Reputation, and Relationships.

4

The First "R": Go for a Great Result

Life is either a daring adventure, or nothing.

Helen Keller

Disconnected influence often leads us, unknowingly, to sell ourselves short. When we focus primarily on getting our way, we often think too narrowly about the best outcome we can convince others to accept —not about getting the best outcome *possible*.

But here's a key lesson we've learned from the people we interviewed: If you're going to influence others, go for something grand. Go for a great outcome. It's ambitious. It's nearly impossible. It's energizing. It's inspiring. It's what could be. It often triggers a response of, "Do you think that's possible?" or "Could we *really* do that?"

Mark often talks about *reverse cognitive bias*, which means that most people wait for things to happen and then react to them. Fewer people have a *forward cognitive bias*—a willingness to engage the challenges and uncertainties that lie ahead. These people, Mark says, ask, "Why settle for an opportunity when you can create and realize a possibility?"

And that's what great outcomes are all about.

When you take the bold step of going for a great outcome, you'll get people to think into their futures. You're not just trying to "trick" them into doing something that's good for you right now. Instead, you're showing them a path to a better **their there**. That's exciting and inspiring—and it leads to creative solutions, great results, and stronger connections with the people you want to influence.

This doesn't mean your great outcome needs to be large. It can be as bold as changing the world, or as simple as raising the bar for how you'll spend the next sixty minutes. It can mean making the most of a conversation, meeting, conference call, presentation, project, or mission. A great outcome doesn't need to be large in scope, but it needs to be rich in meaning . . . and it needs to be great for everyone involved.

Finding your great outcome can be a challenge—especially if you aim high—but the rewards are astonishing. Here are the stories of two "power influencers" who show how it's done.

▪ A Great Outcome for Los Angeles Kids

Finding people's passion is what our friend Ivan Rosenberg is all about. A business consultant, he's helped hundreds of companies and nonprofits find their great outcomes.

A few years ago, Ivan was helping the Alliance for Children's Rights, a nonprofit organization that provides legal services for at-risk children. They were working on their vision and trying out various ideas when one of the team members said, "How about this: 'We're committed to a world in which every child has a safe, loving, and permanent family.'"

The moment he said it, everyone shouted, "Yes!"

Everyone, that is, except for one man. He objected, saying, "Wait, we're just a small Los Angeles organization. We can't change the whole world. It doesn't make sense as a vision. We should focus on Los Angeles."

Ivan said, "It's an important point you're raising, and it goes to the difference between two questions: What do you do vs. what do you stand for?"

"I don't follow," said the man, "What's the difference?"

Ivan said, "Let's talk it through. How would you answer this question: What are you going to stand for?"

The man replied, "We stand for the at-risk kids in Los Angeles County. There are seventy-five thousand of them, and that's a huge number without even going beyond the immediate geographic area. That's more than enough for us to do."

"Okay," said Ivan. "If you don't say something about a topic, you're leaving it to chance, correct? That's not your focus. You're not going to try to influence that."

"Fine," said the man. "Like I said, the kids in Los Angeles County are plenty enough for our small organization to try to handle."

Ivan said, "That means your commitment is "every child in Los Angeles County has a safe, loving and permanent family . . . ""

And here he paused while the man nodded and indicated that sounded fine. Then he went on to add, " and to heck with the rest of them."

"No!" the man objected strongly. "That's not what I mean!"

"So you *do* care about those other kids?" asked Ivan.

"I care very much," he said. "I want every kid in the world to have a safe, loving, and permanent family."

"Of course you do," said Ivan. "*That's* your vision. That's your commitment. That's your passion."

Ivan went on. "That's what you stand for, that's what's in your heart, that's what you want to happen. This organization won't get there on its own, but that's the big picture to which your work contributes. You might focus your efforts on protecting the rights of at-risk children in Los Angeles County, but what you *stand for* is much more than that."

This is going for a great outcome on a grand scale.

As Ivan continued facilitating the group's discussion, they realized that their great outcome fundamentally changed the way they viewed their situation. They used to see themselves in competition for donor dollars with other nonprofit and charity organizations. Now they saw the need to collaborate and coordinate in the service of a common goal.

For example, the group looked at one of their areas of focus—legal services for special needs children, which several other organizations focused on as well. As a group, they determined there was a huge need to support at-risk youth, particularly those in foster care, but it didn't make sense to have several different organizations competing to provide identical services for special needs children. They determined that a better approach, in light of "great outcome" thinking, was to get all these organizations together and figure out how best to make legal services available for *all* of these kids.

So that's what they did. As a coordinated group of organizations, they ended up creating a court panel to which everyone would refer all of their special needs kids. The Alliance for Children's Rights mobilized private resources to build its staff expertise and to leverage the efforts of private law firms all over the city to provide free legal advocacy for the majority of these kids. It saved time and money, and the kids got much needed services. It also catalyzed a new level of communication, coordination, information sharing, and cooperation for all groups concerned with at-risk children.

Ivan gets results like this all the time. And he does it by adding that one missing spark—passion—that takes people from "just getting by" to going for great outcomes.

As Ivan points out, it's not just the doing. It's the *effect* of the doing. It's the excitement that comes from being involved in something that matters. Get the passion piece in place first—find a way for people to make a real difference, and show them how—and you'll drive energy and life into your goals and help turn stale objectives into great outcomes that people want to pursue. Ivan believes that at the end of the day, everyone should be able to say, "That was a day worth giving my life to."

To accomplish such an ambitious goal, you need to be willing to tear down walls and break long-standing rules. That's because going for great outcomes often means getting everyone on your side . . . including your competitors. And that's what our next influencer does best.

■ A Great Outcome at Patagonia

Patagonia, a company that designs outdoor apparel, offers a great line of products. So do lots of other clothing companies. But in addition to fantastic clothes, Patagonia has something most other clothing companies don't: passion.

Patagonia's mission statement includes this great outcome: "Use business to inspire and implement solutions to the environmental crisis." And they mean it.

In pursuit of their commitment to the environment, Patagonia aspires to have *nothing* they ever produce end up in the garbage. It's a simple idea, but think of the implications. *Nothing ends up in the garbage.*

It's a massively ambitious aspiration. It's inspiring. It's a great outcome.

And no one is more passionate about that great outcome than Jill Dumain, director of environmental strategy at Patagonia. With a staff of just two people, she encourages everyone in the company to "own" this mission statement. Ideas pour into her office, spread throughout the company, and then go out to the world as she openly shares what Patagonia is learning about efficient, environmentally sound processes.

In addition, Jill is spearheading an effort to encourage the entire apparel industry to use the Eco Index, a tool that allows companies to determine the environmental impact of their products and processes. It's open source, so anyone can easily adopt it.

One person told us, "Jill is remarkably sincere and transparent. Even though we're competitors, she worked with me about sustainability and responsible sourcing for our suppliers. She did it with others, too, and completely changed their outlook. Normally with retailers, everyone is protective, but that changed with Jill. She opened us up. She taught me and other retailers that we can compete but also be cooperative. She'd say, 'We want to tell you as much as possible so you can get ahead on how to reduce water usage, and on using dyes and chemicals effectively, and being more energy efficient. We all share common goals on what affects the environment.'

"Then she would back it up. She'll always go first, sharing what she's learned, teaching us best practices, and putting us in touch with experts in her network. She'll come back from weeks of research, meetings, and deep immersion into a region, or a material, or a production process, and then give everything away. We get the fruits of her expertise, relationships, and hard work for free. She lives the bigger picture, and that's persuasive. It's inspiring. You *want* to listen to her. You *want* to get on board, because she helps others see themselves as part of a larger whole, a meaningful mission."

Essentially, Jill has unilaterally redefined her role, extending it to achieve the company's core value: doing good business in ways that help protect the environment. Because of her passion, she influences decision makers around the world. And because of her efforts, every person who works at Patagonia can leave work at the end of the day and honestly say, "Today, we helped create and sell a great product . . . and we helped save the world."

One message of Jill's story is that a great outcome doesn't have to require a huge investment. At Patagonia, she accomplishes her great outcome with a staff of only two people. That's because by expanding her focus to include everyone in her company and even her competitors, she's expanded her influence exponentially.

But another message is that it takes both vision and hard work to influence people positively in a big way. And more than that, it requires what one of Jill's admirers calls "strategic patience." Often, Jill spends weeks or months getting people to the table. She listens to them without giving in; she empathizes without compromising her standards; and she builds relationships to advance the long-term good, even if short-term wins fall short. She creates the space for amazing things to happen . . . and often, they do.

Casey Sheahan, CEO of Patagonia, notes that Jill has a saying taped to her desk that reads: "Encourage, Entice, and Inspire." "That's exactly what she does," he said. "That's how she creates a ripple effect throughout people in the company and then outside to other companies, and then to global impact on the planet."

And that's truly a great outcome.

Jill is just one of the many power influencers we met who are creating great outcomes by bringing different groups to the table. Another is Jim Schroer, a partner at Next Autoworks—a pioneering car company that strives to increase innovation and cut costs by fostering collaboration among suppliers, dealers, and customers. Their great outcome is producing five-star, crash-proof, fuel-efficient, affordable cars.

Jim says that getting people to sign on to this unprecedented collaboration is all about convincing them that his company is guided by good motives.

For instance, when Next Autoworks asks vendors for ideas, the venders often respond, "No other manufacturer has asked us that before. But are you going to undermine us? Take our ideas and then turn around and bid the job out to other vendors?" Jim's team replies, "We want to listen to your ideas. We want to work together. We want you to come out okay so we can create a working relationship that works for all of us—customers, vendors, manufacturers." The vendors sign on to this ambitious outcome—one that's likely to lead to safer, better, and less expensive cars for all of us.

▶ *Usable Insight*

Imagine what it would mean for you to reach for the standard Ivan suggests: "At the end of the day, that was a day worth giving my life to." How would that affect your planning for the day, the priorities you set, how you spend your time at work and at home, how you handle unexpected challenges and difficulties, and how you interact with the people around you?

▶ *Action Steps*

Think of a cause you're passionate about that aligns with your organization. Identify the people in your organization or industry who are likely to share your passion for this mission and who can help multiply its impact. Then strategize how to make it happen. And consider expanding your reach by working with other teams, other departments, or even your competitors to make your great outcome a reality.

Now, do the same thing in your personal life. Think of a cause you care deeply about, and identify the friends and family members who'd be willing to join you in creating a great outcome.

If you're finding it hard to clarify the great outcome you want to pursue, try the "What's your sentence?" exercise created by Dan Pink, author of the best seller, *Drive: The Surprising Truth About What Motivates Us*. Think about what your life is about and what you want to do with it. Then distill your answer into a single sentence—for instance, "He improved the quality of life for children with disabilities," or "She created software that allowed doctors to provide better care for patients."

5

The Second "R":
Go for a Great
Reputation

It takes twenty years to build a reputation and five minutes to ruin it.
If you think about that, you'll do things differently.

Warren Buffett

One big reason why disconnected influence is very tempting is because it's easy. You don't need to care about the aftereffects of people's buy-in, because you aren't planning to stick around to see what happens next. If your actions hurt or disappoint them, you won't care. And if they need your help, that's too bad—because you'll be long gone.

Connected influence, however, requires you to prove that you're worthy of people's long-term commitment. To get people to support your great outcomes, you need to support *them* . . . even when it's not in your best short-term interest. They need to know that you're committed to their success as well as yours. And they need to know that if they're in trouble, you'll stand up for them, even if the cost is high. In short, you need to be a hero.

The actions you take to help others—or the actions you decline to take—can make or break connections forever. To understand just how powerful these choices are, do this quick exercise:

1. Think about a time when you were in a very difficult situation.
2. Think about the people who were aware of your situation.
3. Think about what each of these people did (or didn't do) in response to your situation.
4. Identify the people who put themselves on the line financially or otherwise took a risk to help you.
5. Identify the people who came to your aid even though they themselves received no benefit from helping you.
6. Identify the people who stood up to you to prevent you from doing something they knew you would regret.
7. Describe how these people's actions affected your life.

Nearly everyone we ask to do this exercise identifies a core group of people who supported them during their worst times. Often, these people had no real obligation to help—and sometimes, they took a significant risk in doing so.

When we ask the people in our audiences if these are the same people who influence them today, they respond with a heartfelt "yes." They tell us that these are the people they are proud to follow, willing to support, and honored to help in any way possible. What's more, our respondents are excited to have an opportunity to spread the word about these people. Unlike the effects of disconnected influence, this kind of gratitude doesn't come with an expiration date.

Over and over, people tell us that the men and women who influenced them the most weren't the ones who persuaded them to do things. Instead, they were the ones who deeply cared about them and showed it. As one man put it, "This person was committed to not letting me fail."

So when you're going for great outcomes, commit to standing up for everyone who helps to make your dreams a reality. Be willing to support them for better or for worse, and to inspire them by being there when they need you. And be aware that connected influence is not for sissies . . . as Jim Clark and Larry Clark can prove.

▧ Jim Clark's Story

Long before he became president of western operations for Prudential Insurance, Jim Clark was a district manager in suburban Chicago. He heard about a man named Larry Clark (no relation) who managed a large department store in a suburb called Chicago Heights. Prudential agents and their wives frequented the store and referred everyone to it because people loved doing business with Larry.

Jim, always on the lookout for talent, was eager to meet someone with such a strong reputation. When he did meet Larry, he saw what everyone else saw—a man of immense talent, integrity, and skill. Jim immediately decided on a great outcome: Even if it seemed impossible, he would get Larry to join his team. So he began a personal campaign to recruit Larry into Prudential.

There were two big obstacles. One was that Larry was in an excellent position and was doing well as department store manager. The other obstacle was that Larry was African-American, and there were no African-American insurance agents in any suburban districts in the entire organization in 1965. In fact, when he set out to recruit Larry, Jim met strong resistance from his own colleagues solely because Larry was black.

Jim knew he could overcome this resistance. But first, he had to win Larry over.

Larry says that Jim would come out to his store in Chicago Heights every week and take him to lunch. Larry kept saying, "Jim, I don't need to come to Prudential. I have a good job here." Jim would say "That's fine," and then come back again next week, and they would go out for coffee and pie together.

For nine months, Jim came every week. He got to know Larry, his situation at work, his goals, and his concerns. He came to Larry's home and met his wife. He got to know Larry's mother and father. He got to know Larry's in-laws and met with community leaders that Larry knew. Jim had Larry and his wife over to his home to meet his wife and children.

Then it happened. One day Larry asked for an extra hour off on a Friday afternoon because he wasn't feeling well. His boss said it would have to wait until Monday because there was a sale going on.

"But I feel sick and I can hardly swallow," said Larry, who later found out he had strep throat.

His boss said, "You still have to wait until Monday."

In two years of being a manager, Larry had quadrupled the sales in his department. In seven and a half years of working at the store, he had taken only two days off—the day his daughter was born, and the day his grandmother died.

That was it. He called Jim Clark.

When Larry said he was leaving the company, they tried to get him back. They offered him part ownership in the store, a large bonus, and help with buying a house.

Larry said no. "You treated me like gum on the floor."

When Larry's moment of truth arrived, he knew where to turn. That's because he knew Jim could use his skills—and he knew that Jim, unlike his former boss, was a man of integrity.

Larry says, "Jim never wavered in his confidence in me. There were problems with people accepting a black person into the office. But Jim held firm. It was very bold of him. His reputation was on the line. He had to handle the adversity that would be thrown toward him."

Larry went looking for a house and encountered prejudice. In one city, they raised the price from $30,000 and a ten percent down payment for white buyers to $49,000 and a fifteen percent down payment for him. So he went to another city. Larry says, "The agent saw us coming and hid in the closet. I opened the door and the guy went down on his knees. He thought we were going to beat him up. I told him, 'You can get up. I know what your answer is.'"

So Jim went to bat for Larry again. He encouraged Larry to buy a house in his own neighborhood in a city called Park Forest, where Jim could personally endorse Larry. At first it looked promising. Larry found a place for $29,000 and a ten percent down payment.

"That was in my range," said Larry. "But then the agent kept coming up with excuses to raise the down payment, which started at $2,900. When it got up to $8,000, that was my absolute limit. I would only have thirty-five dollars left in my bank account."

He told Jim who said, "Don't worry about the down payment, whatever it is. Sign the papers, and whatever you don't have, I'll make up the difference." Jim also gave him a $500 check to deposit in his bank account to cover any other expenses. Larry bought the house and returned the uncashed check three weeks later after getting paid in his new job.

Jim also mentored Larry by showing him everything he knew about the business and how to be successful at it. Within two years, Larry was number one in sales out of 3,200 sales managers in the company—and as district manager, Jim was number one in sales out of 560 districts.

It was a great outcome—and it took enormous integrity on Jim's part. Jim responded each time challenges arose, standing up for Larry in the face of ugly office gossip and prejudice and helping encourage him through the incredibly difficult process of buying a home. He even opened his own wallet to help out.

At any point, he could have abandoned Larry to deal with these problems on his own. But he didn't—and as a result, he achieved even more great outcomes. He forced Prudential to confront its prejudices. He brought in one of the highest achievers ever to work at the company. And he created a bond with Larry that lasts to this day.

In short, Jim was a hero. And so, as the next story shows, was Larry.

■ Larry's Story

Larry grew up in the Midwest in the 1950s and 1960s, when overt prejudice was still commonplace and widely supported in institutions. Where Larry went to high school, black students were not permitted to go to the dance hall. They could not bowl in local bowling alleys—they had to drive forty miles to get to a place that allowed them to enter. They could not swim in the local pools. They could not stay in the hotels and motels. When they went on trips, they had to sleep in cars. (As a footnote, Larry says, "I'm indebted to Holiday Inn, which was the first to let blacks in without fanfare. As I traveled through the south, I always felt welcome and safe there.")

In 1965, Larry was the first black person invited to join the Kiwanis Club in his area. At that time, Kiwanis was still sponsoring blackface minstrel shows, in which white entertainers would put dark polish on their faces and ridicule black people.

The first meeting Larry attended featured a blackface minstrel performance. Larry says, "I stood up and said I have to make a statement, and maybe I'll get thrown out. But if you have to make money by degrading a segment of society, something is wrong." An uproar ensued. Larry said, "They had been doing this maybe for one hundred years, but many people were there who knew me, and they stood up and said, 'He's right. It's time we stopped this.' And that was the end of it."

Throughout his career, there were people who stood up for Larry and others who explicitly tried to subvert his success and discredit him. Some executives once tried to put him on probation for made-up reasons. He challenged the charges immediately and directly. He went straight to the reviewing official in person and said, "If I fail to rebut these charges, I will tender my resignation today. If I successfully rebut them, I'd like to know what you will do." Larry says, "He wouldn't answer, but he looked at the information and said it was ridiculous and dismissed the charges. I asked, 'What do you think their motives are? Incompetent or prejudiced, or both?' He didn't answer that question either. But soon the person who brought the false charges was demoted, and another executive who pushed the charges abruptly took early retirement."

Larry could easily have pursued a lawsuit, and in fact he was approached by a nationally reputable organization that estimated his possible settlement at twelve to fourteen million dollars—an enormous sum, especially in those days. But Larry declined to sue. He told us that he thought about it at great length and concluded, "If I pursued the lawsuit at that time, under those conditions, it was likely that the minorities I brought into the business would have suffered greatly. Their clients in those days might well have discontinued their insurance. It was a purpose of mine to help the careers of minority agents, and I thought that lawsuit could hurt them."

Others in management tried to create one hundred percent black offices. He was told, "Black people should manage black people." Larry strongly objected, saying "Either you're qualified or not. Would you say an Italian manager should only work with Italians?"

One striking incident occurred when Larry was receiving his first award as the number one sales manager in the company. "It was at the Mid-America Club," he says, "at that time one of the most prestigious restaurants in Chicago, at the top of the Prudential building. Hundreds of people were there. I was announced as the recipient and started to walk up to the front of the audience when a guy named Walter said, in a very loud voice, 'Hey Larry, what are you going to do with that big front yard of yours, plant watermelons in it?'"

A hush came over the room.

Larry remained calm. "Walter, as long as I'm associated with you," he said, "I'll never have an inferiority complex."

Walter got so mad he threw his glass across the room.

Ironically, not long afterward, Walter's son, who was also employed by Prudential, was placed in Larry's organization. Larry didn't hold it against him. Walter's son performed very well, and Larry promoted him as one of his first sales managers.

Larry says, "Years later Walter came in to the office and wanted to see me. He had tears in his eyes, and said, 'Thank you so much for helping my son. I gave you pure hell back then, and I'm sorry. The best thing that ever happened to my son was working for you.'"

Jim and Larry built their reputations by standing up for their principles even when things got tough. And they burnished those reputations by standing up for the people involved in their great outcomes: Jim, by going the extra mile for Larry; and Larry, by fighting for the minority agents who followed him into Prudential . . . and by giving Walter's son a chance to prove that he was a better man than his father.

Like them, you can strengthen your reputation through extraordinary conduct under challenging conditions. But you can also enhance it in quiet but powerful ways by taking a stand for someone you value.

For instance, Mark tells this story about how a personal hero of his came through for him during one of the worst times of his life:

"There is no better way to be influenced than to be vulnerable and have the great fortune to be in the presence of a loving and caring person. For me, that person was Dean William McNary, dean of students at Boston University School of Medicine, who was there when I hit rock bottom.

"After one-and-a-half years in medical school my mind stopped, or at least the part of my mind I needed to function in medical school. I was highlighting all my books in yellow, hoping that by osmosis the facts, the tables, the information would go in and stay in. The osmosis didn't happen.

"Miraculously I was still passing, as our grading system had gone to pass-or-fail. But I didn't want to become a doctor and put my patients at risk by not knowing anything. I asked for and received a leave of absence, and went out and took some blue-collar jobs that didn't require thinking at the level of medical school.

"I felt restored to normal after that year, and I returned to medical school. But then all the 'brain fog' came back, and by the end of a mere six months I was a wreck again. Again I was still passing, and again I asked for a leave of absence.

"Now, what you may not know is that the tuition medical students pay is nowhere near the cost of educating them, and the government provides supplemental funds. If a spot goes unfilled (as when someone takes a leave of absence), the school loses those funds. And here I was, causing the school to again take a financial hit.

"The dean of the medical school set up an appointment to see me. Unlike the dean of students, the dean of the school was more concerned with the school's financial challenges than with any student's personal issues.

"A week later, Dean McNary—or Mac, as he was called—
asked me to come to his office. Mac, who had a deep Irish
Catholic accent, invited me to sit down in his office and said:
'M-a-h-k, I have a letter here from the dean of the school that I
think you need to read.' He handed it to me.

"In essence it said, 'I have met with Mr. Goulston to discuss
his situation, and in the time it would take him to finish medical
school, an internship, and residency, he could learn an entirely
different career that he could succeed at—perhaps even playing
the cello, to which he agreed. So I hereby request that the
Promotions Committee ask Mr. Goulston to withdraw.'

"I was confused and said, 'I don't remember this, and I
certainly don't remember agreeing to anything—especially
learning to play the cello. What does this mean?'

"That's when Mac said to me calmly and concisely, 'It means
you have been kicked out.'

"I felt like I'd been shot. My shoulders dropped, then my
head. Then the air went out of me, and in about twenty seconds
I felt as if I was bleeding from my eyes.

"Mac patiently waited for me to regain my senses and then
with a knowing smile said, 'Mahk, I know you didn't say those
things, you're too screwed up to agree to anything. Look, you
didn't screw up (he noted that I was still passing everything),
but you *are* screwed up. But I believe that if you got unscrewed
up, this school would one day be glad they gave you a *second*
chance.' My tears poured out, because I'd been injected with a
dollop of caring that enabled me for the first time in my life to
experience basic trust at my core.

"Mac then asked me to look at him and said: 'You deserve to
be on this planet—and the reason for that, and the reason you
deserve a second chance, is that you have a core of kindness and
goodness and you have no idea how valuable and necessary to

the world that is. And you won't know until you're thirty-five. Your challenge is to make it to thirty-five to find it out.'

"Mac waited for me to regain my composure. And then just as firmly as he'd spoken before, he said: 'Mahk, will you *please* let me help you?' It wasn't a request; it was close to a demand—as if he intuitively knew that if he'd said, 'Call me if I can be of help,' I would have thanked him and never asked for it. It was if he grabbed me by scruff of my neck and was telling me, 'I'm not going to let you go.'

"At that point, I got embarrassed and looked away, but then limply replied, 'I think I'd like that.'

"Mac then arranged an appeal to the promotions committee regarding the 'done deal' decision to have me leave. This was not an easy thing to do, because he was 'just' a Ph.D., and the promotions committee was comprised of top department heads from both the medical school and related hospitals. He told me that he would get me in the door, but I would have to make my case to them directly.

"I did plead my case and explained what had happened to me. Several doctors were sympathetic, but it wasn't going well because the final questioning fell to the head of the committee who was a cigar-chomping head of the surgery department at the largest Boston hospital and an individual who was smart, blunt, and universally disliked. He heard me and then barked at me: 'Look, you really don't seem to be someone who could or should become a doctor. Doctors need to be confident and decisive and you just aren't. So tell me, why should we give you another chance?'

"I noted that I'd gotten divorced after a very short marriage; my father had had colon cancer; and I had had Graves' Disease and had received medications that made me hypothyroid to the point that I needed to be injected with thyroxine so I could stay awake in class. I was so confused that I didn't know if those were even legitimate excuses. I said that I didn't know if I wanted to be a doctor, but I also didn't know if I didn't want to be a doctor.

"At that point the head of the committee fired back at me cigar in hand: 'Yeah, yeah,' and then repeated, 'And so why should we give you another chance?'

"I don't know what got into me, but I looked him squarely in the eye and blurted something out that was dramatic but was ironically very real, 'And *so* I'd like to plead insanity and throw myself on the mercy of a group of physicians.'

"At that point the head of the committee smashed his cigar out in an ashtray, turned his seat around with his back facing me, and crossed his arms in silence.

"Nobody spoke in the room for five minutes. Then Mac told me I was excused and that they would discuss my case. I went out and sat in a stairwell with my arms around the cold metal of the staircase. After fifteen minutes, Mac came out, sat down next to me, and said, 'Mahk, take one year, take five years, you will always be welcome back at Boston University School of Medicine.'

"I took that year off and went to the Menninger Foundation and did a stint as a medical student at Topeka State Hospital. I might not have been medical school material but the psychiatrists there told me, 'You really seem to have a knack at getting through to and influencing schizophrenic farm boys. You could be good at this.'

"I did return to medical school, graduated, and went on to study psychiatry at UCLA; and I have been 'paying it forward' by influencing people to find hope, success, and meaning in their lives ever since.

"About ten years after this happened, I visited Boston to take Mac out to lunch. I asked him why he'd gone out on a limb for me. He smiled and said, 'Thirty years ago someone did it for me. And that is why all I've wanted to do was be dean of students and help people like you.'

"As an epilogue to the story, my wife and I named our first son, Billy, after him."

Jim Clark, Larry Clark, and "Mac" McNary all built their reputations in different ways. But no matter how you build your own good reputation—through public gestures or behind-the-scenes support—it will empower you to wield positive influence both with the people you help and with the people *they* influence.

A strong reputation will make people want to work with you, want to deal with you, want to listen to you, and want to help you. Because of what they've heard and learned about you, they will anticipate that good things will happen, even before they meet you. And, as our three heroes demonstrate, that can turn great outcomes into extraordinary ones.

▶ *Usable Insight*

How would it affect your approach to influencing others if the people you interact with this week were going to post a video next week—online for anyone to see, forever—about the way you've treated them?

▶ *Action Step*

The inspiration for this step comes from Jonathan Fitzgarrald, chief marketing officer for the law firm, Greenberg Glusker Fields Claman & Machtinger LLP, who tells the story of how his parents used to take him and his five siblings out to dinner. His father, Ike, would let them reach a certain level of noisiness and then lean forward and in a loud whisper, say, "People are watching!" Jonathan says his dad's example taught him that "everything we say (and don't say) and do (and don't do) communicates something about us to those around us."

To open your eyes to the messages you're sending to the people around you, try this exercise. For an entire week, make a point of observing your own actions from other people's **there** when you're at work, out in public, or at home. Then ask yourself:

- What did you communicate by what you said and did?
- What did you communicate by what you *didn't* say and do?
- How do you think your actions affected your reputation?

6

The Third "R": Go for Great Relationships

In real estate it's "location, location, location."
In healthcare it's "relationship, relationship, relationship."
Pat Sweeney, former senior vice president at McKesson Corporation

Disconnected influence steers us into thinking solely about getting results. But when that keeps us from thinking about building relationships, a very peculiar thing happens: We often get worse results.

Of course, results *are* important to consider—tasks completed, projects accomplished, budgets approved, and sales achieved. Results stand out. They get attention. They're easy to measure, publish, and verify.

Results also lend themselves to scorekeeping because they're more visible than the emotional math of relationships. But more visible doesn't mean more important. Relationships aren't always evident, but they *always* have an effect. If you damage your relationships, people will be less willing to support your great outcomes and might even work to undermine them.

Of course, there's not anything wrong with reaching for results.

That's why we say you should go beyond "doable" goals and aim for inspiring ones. But if you focus too narrowly on getting results at the expense of building relationships, you may achieve neither.

As an illustration, how many times have you seen someone embarrass or belittle others publicly and unnecessarily—for example, by making sarcastic remarks behind other people's backs about their mistakes or shortcomings? If you think about it, you'll realize that you silently lost some respect for the perpetrator of those remarks, even if the person got a laugh in the room. Even if *you* laughed at the time.

Moreover, it probably made you stop and wonder later on: "Does this person say similar things about me behind my back?" Most likely, that question stayed in the back of your mind, making you trust the person less and feel less willing to connect and open up honestly. That kind of distrust can throw huge roadblocks in the path of great outcomes.

Conversely, people who invest in relationships get everyone to buy into their great outcomes. For instance, John worked for several years with Mel Hall, the former CEO and chairman of Press Ganey Associates. He remembers the first day he met with Mel at the Press Ganey headquarters. As they walked around, they'd encounter people randomly in the halls. Mel knew everyone's first name. He introduced each one of them to John, telling him what their role was and how long they'd worked with the company (he knew that too), and mentioning something special about their contributions.

"They are the ones who make the difference," Mel would say. "If you really believe that, that they are the source of competitive advantage, then it's imperative that you know about them."

All of the powerful influencers we've talked with believe in this philosophy. They know that strong relationships make other people want to listen and buy in, rather than being suspicious or adversarial.

But building strong relationships with the people you want on your side takes mindfulness and effort. Here's a look at how our influencers put their philosophy into action every day.

◼ Rocking Relationships

Joey Gold has one of the strangest résumés of anyone we know: He's a rock star turned aerospace engineer.

Joey's done everything from opening for Ozzy Osbourne (a story we'll get to in Chapter Ten) to managing technical projects for a major international aerospace firm, and he's a master at creating great outcomes. In addition, he's one of the most "connected" influencers we've met, and his story shows that positive influence gets great results no matter what career you're in.

Joey says, "I've always valued people and treated people with the utmost respect. On the road, I knew everyone's names—the roadies, the t-shirt vendors, the promoters, the other bands, the security, the bus drivers, the ushers—everyone. To me, it was one big organism and everyone was needed and valued, and everyone needed to be treated with respect. I appreciated them and wanted them to feel appreciated."

He adds, "It's the same now at work. I know the executives, their administrative assistants, the person who vacuums my office and takes out my trash—everyone. I'm nice to everyone and it isn't fake. I truly like everyone. Everyone has value, and I do what I can for people. I spend a fortune on See's Candy at the end of the year and write cards to all of the assistants, people who do the office moves, security, and people who help with sanitation. I do it because I want to, not because I want something out of them."

Joey gets treated well at work, and he makes sure his team does, too. "I get an office for someone on my team when it wasn't available at first," he says. "I get items ordered for my team when there's supposedly a backlog of orders."

Joey says he gets support not because he gives out See's Candy but because people know his respect for them is genuine. "It was the same when I was in music," he says. "I was the 'nice guy' in Hollywood—the one who didn't do drugs, lie, and steal your girlfriend. I treated people well, and I think it helped me and the band to get treated well, and it got us out of some tough spots. But I didn't treat people well then or now to get them to do something for me."

Instead, he says, "I try to treat people well because it's a better way to live and it was the example my father showed me. As it turns out, it's led to success I wouldn't have imagined in music, battling back from cancer, going back to school for an undergraduate degree in mathematics, getting graduate degrees in electrical engineering and management, achieving a terrific second career in aerospace, and having an incredible wife and family. I'm blessed, and I'd be ashamed not to treat people well."

For Joey, strong relationships are integral to achieving great outcomes. It's a philosophy our next influencer also lives by—and in fact, she believes in it so strongly that one of her great outcomes is based on building bonds.

■ Elevator Pitches vs. Vulnerability Pitches

Debbie Quintana is an innovator in the gift basket industry. She made the prestigious "40 under 40" list for Silicon Valley, and won the 2011 Silicon Valley Women of Influence Award.

Debbie is the CEO of The Best Gourmet Gifts, a gift basket company that's been driving significant change in that industry. For example, she pioneered the concept of letting customers watch live on video while their custom gift basket is being put together so they can make changes if they want. She also created a Gift Basket Association and an industry-leading magazine.

Debbie drives for results, but she's also a natural relationship builder. However, when she decided to get involved with professional networking groups in her region, she couldn't find what she was looking for.

If Debbie can't find something, she makes it herself. So she created the Women's Networking Alliance, which now has nine chapters in the United States and is adding a tenth in Australia.

"I wasn't looking for a place where it's all about collecting leads and referrals," she says. "I didn't want elevator pitches, I wanted vulnerability pitches. I wanted a place where it was about growing as a person and a businessperson. I wanted it to be about sharing challenges, talking about where we need help, being open, and not being judged or evaluated."

The alliance keeps chapter sizes small, and they're highly selective about adding members. They look for people who care about other people and demonstrate that concern through their actions.

"It's not for everyone," Debbie says, "but that's fine with us. I'd rather have five people there for the right reasons than forty for the wrong reasons. I want real relationships.

"Instead of posturing and preening," Debbie says, "people get vulnerable. It's not so much about *how great I am*, but *where I need help*. We don't do fake. We don't do 'pretend.' Sure, we have fun and laugh, but we're also not afraid to get down to the ugly stuff. We show weakness, and we ask for help, even if it's hard, even if it's embarrassing."

Debbie offers an example. "Someone might say, 'I don't know how to use Facebook and I'm embarrassed about it. In fact, I'm so technology challenged I'm not sure I can continue my business. I don't understand it and I'm falling further behind and I'm afraid.'

"Then we rally around that person. Or we ask questions like, 'What attribute or characteristic do you want to improve on, and why?' Every year we give inspiration awards, which are about personal qualities, facing fear, character, and commitment."

The people in this unique networking group do gain powerful professional benefits from their participation. But those results aren't the primary point. Results come, but they come from being with relationship-oriented people in a relationship-building environment.

BUILDING RELATIONSHIPS THE ZAPPOS WAY

Tony Hsieh, CEO of the hugely successful online shoe company, Zappos.com, offers a view on building relationships that's very similar to Debbie Quintana's. In his book, *Delivering Happiness*, Tony writes:

> I personally really dislike business networking events . . . . Instead, I really prefer to focus on just building relationships and getting to know people as just people, regardless of their position in the business world or even if they're not from the business world.
>
> I believe that there's something interesting about anyone and everyone. You just have to figure out what that something is. If anything, I've found that it's more interesting to build relationships with people that are not in the business world, because they almost always can offer unique perspectives and insights and also because those relationships tend to be more genuine.
>
> If you're able to figure out how to be truly interested in someone you meet, with the goal of striking up a friendship, instead of trying to get something out of that person, the

funny thing is, almost always, something happens later down the line that ends up either benefiting your business or yourself personally. I don't really know why this happens or why it works, but it seems that the benefit from getting to know someone on a personal level usually happens two to three years after you started working on building the relationship, and it's usually something that you could not have possibly predicted would have happened at the beginning of the relationship.

For Debbie and Tony, great networking outcomes don't start with a transactional relationship—"Pass my business card on to your boss, and I'll recommend your software to mine." And they don't start with a focus on results (although the results are often amazing). Instead, they begin with transformational relationships in which people share their strengths, open up about their vulnerabilities, unselfishly offer assistance, and build ties that don't begin and end with business cards.

Because of their commitment to building real relationships, Debbie and Tony are revered as "super mentors," with hundreds of mentees multiplying their influence. But as our next influencer shows, you can build remarkable relationships in a very different way by asking people to mentor *you*.

■ Teaming Up with the "Fat Brains"

Gina Rudan, author of *Practical Genius*, has a catchy label for people between the ages of twenty and thirty-five. She calls them "fat brains." (That's because at that stage of life, people ostensibly have more fat content in their brains than at later ages.) Fat brains, Gina says, are young, energetic, committed, forward-thinking people.

They are more technologically adept than their older counterparts, want to make a difference, are bold and creative in solving problems and integrating work and play, and above all, aren't afraid to try new things.

Gina says that everyone should have several fat brains in their lives. She herself has over a dozen she counts not only as good friends but as "reverse mentors."

She says, "I stumbled upon this notion when I quit my corporate job to start my own practice at the start of the last recession. I knew I had to surround myself with people who were living, breathing, and acting from the fringe and that meant entrepreneurs. I had to adopt a new tribe."

She attended a retreat held at a ranch in Texas by a young entrepreneur named Dan Lack, who called it "The Meeting of the Big Minds." Gina says, "There were young thought leaders, some of them starting businesses, others launching nonprofits. I knew I had found my new tribe."

She began to journal about what she'd learned by opening up to people half her age. "At one point I asked Dan to be my mentor and he laughed," says Gina. "I said, 'I'm serious, I'm going to look for your leadership and guidance about what I should be reading and conferences I should be attending, and we're going to have a nontransactional relationship.'"

That was three years ago. "In a lot of ways, we couldn't be more different," Gina says. "He's a young Jewish male, and a southern guy. I'm a Puerto Rican woman from New York. But the relationship blossomed. With my husband and son, we've essentially merged families with Dan and his relatives. We visit and interact with each other's families. People say, 'I can't believe you spend so much time with twenty-five-year-olds!' My husband is fifty, I'm forty, and Dan Lack is really part of my family now."

Because of Gina, Dan has a second family of people who go

out of their way to support him. And thanks to Dan, Gina learns about music, trends, technology, and social media. She also learns how to combine working and playing, problem solving and socializing.

"It's something I didn't get nearly as much in my previous career," Gina says. "Having 'work' discussions in social environments: on beaches, in fringe coffee houses, at concerts, in my backyard. They do it without thinking about it. Business meetings and social meetings for them are the same. They look for experience and environment in everything they do. I find it to be an innovative approach that allows you to gain different perspectives, thought stimulation, and motivation."

She also says she values her young mentor's extreme determination. "Folks our age get exhausted easier," she says. "But they are relentless. They never give up."

Gina is changing her life by letting her tribe of young people teach her how they think, work, see life, and understand trends. As a result, at an age when many of us tend to start settling into a middle-aged rut, she's constantly evolving, both personally and professionally. In return, she's sharing her professional experience, knowledge, and talents with a new generation. That's a great outcome . . . both for her and for her "fat brain" tribe.

> While we're on the topic of relationships, we'd like to introduce you to two more powerful influencers who've fostered their reputations by making introductions.
>
> Jeanine "Nini" Martin, a director of national healthcare for Avanade, Inc., built her strong standing in her industry on a foundation of steady introductions. She says, "I'm one hundred percent relationship driven. I will invest months if not years in relationships, and I don't even have 'asks.'" She says that

people call her "The Connecter," adding with characteristic humility: "I'm Nini the nobody, but I have the ability to connect 'somebodies.'" That ability has helped to establish her as a trusted adviser to state and local governments, medical academia, enterprise commercial firms, and independent physician associations.

Similarly, Michael Altman, of Simon, Altman & Kabaker Financial & Insurance Services, is legendary for connecting people one-at-a-time. He says his secret is no secret. "Whenever I meet someone, I try to learn about them, and think of whom I know who can help them. It's that simple."

How seriously does Michael take this goal? For many years, he's made it his mission to make at least one introduction a day before noon.

■ Playing the Longer Game

Like our other power influencers, David Heinemeier Hansson—partner at the innovative productivity software firm, 37signals—knows that building relationships is more important than always getting his own way.

"Decisions are temporary," David says. "Oftentimes the most important thing is not to be right. We make very few decisions that are so important that the criticality of them being right is so high. We care more about the long-term batting averages of our positions. I try to allow other people to win arguments."

For instance, he says, in earlier years they were deciding whether to ask for credit card information from customers at the beginning or at the end of the trial period for using the software. "I thought, let's keep it up front. Others said it would make a massive difference to push it out until after the trial. My hypothesis was it wasn't true and would be a waste of time. We'd spend two weeks developing the capability, and that would be a waste." But a group of people felt passionate about it, so David and Jason Fried (the president of 37signals, and co-author with David of the book, *Rework*) told them to go for it.

David explains, "We were playing the longer game. Why should I use a veto in a situation like this? It would likely undermine their enthusiasm, responsibility, and ownership. And we can change it back later anyway. We can test it. We can be open to ideas like this. Even if it doesn't work, it might cost a bit in terms of resources, but we'll all learn, and they'll be more engaged and motivated. They'll be more interested in the work, and care about the well-being of the organization."

David adds, "Of course there is one more thing. I could be wrong." And in fact, if you go to the website today, you'll find that you can sign up for a free trial without providing your credit card information until the end of the trial. So his colleagues weren't just passionate; they were right.

David also didn't think that having an illustration-based design for the company's home page would work. But instead of saying no, he decided to run an experiment for a week, and then go back to the old way. "But there was a huge increase in signups," says David. "I was wrong, and the person who proposed it was right. If you treat people the right way, you win whether you're right or wrong on an issue."

By choosing to play the longer game rather than forcing people to do what he wanted, David has helped to build an enormously successful business. And simultaneously, he built strong relationships with a network of dedicated colleagues who know they're valued and who want to add value in return.

BUILDING RELATIONSHIPS WHEN YOU'VE REACHED THE TOP

One key message of this book is that even if you begin with few connections and little money, you can become a power influencer. But here's something else that's crucial to remember: When you reach the pinnacle of influence, your work in building and strengthening relationships still isn't done.

Risa Lavizzo-Mourey, MD, MBA, is president of the Robert Wood Johnson Foundation, the largest philanthropy focused solely on health and healthcare in the United States. With $9 billion in assets, the foundation generates approximately $350 million in grants every year. Their positive influence as an organization is enormous.

Dr. Lavizzo-Mourey says, "Our mission is to improve health and healthcare, yet we can't mandate social change. We don't make policy, we don't deliver services, we don't produce healthcare products. We produce information. We engage with people. We influence. That's what we do. That and our reputation are our biggest capital."

Right now, the foundation is focusing on a great outcome: conquering childhood obesity. Dr. Lavizzo-Mourey says it will take at least a generation to reverse the obesity epidemic. To accomplish this goal, she says, "We look for ways to make it nonpartisan or at least bipartisan—get both parties at all levels of government speaking out." In addition, she's bringing together people from all walks of life—from religious leaders to food manufacturers and retailers—to create healthier outcomes for America's children.

■ Take the R&R Test

The relationships we've focused on in this chapter are the third element of the three "R"s that lead to great outcomes. These three elements aren't mutually exclusive. In fact, it's just the opposite.

All three of these "R"s—results, reputation, relationships—are inescapably interconnected. Over time, and sometimes immediately, the three "R"s catch up with each other. In particular, results achieved by self-serving means will ultimately damage a person's reputation and relationships. And when that happens, the chance for a great outcome is gone.

This is why the most influential people in our experience think about long-term implications even in their short-term actions. They drive for results, but they care about how they get those results. They don't make trade-offs between getting things done and earning trust and confidence with every interaction. The people around them know that they're not merely the means to the influencer's ends, but crucially important ends in their own right.

However, as we've noted, it's extremely easy to fall into focusing on *results* at the expense of the other two "R"s. In fact, this is the core mistake that disconnected influencers make. And it takes mindful effort to break this bad habit.

Here's a daily mental exercise we recommend to help you keep these two easily overlooked "R"s front and center at all times. We call this the "R&R Test."

THE R&R TEST

BEFORE you find yourself interacting with another person or group, ask yourself: How can I strive to build relationships and create a basis for a positive reputation in this interaction?

DURING your interaction, ensure that all of your actions meet these standards: Will what I'm about to say or do increase people's trust and respect and my own credibility? If what I'm about to say or do were being recorded on video and audio, would I be proud to have others whose opinions matter to me see the recording?

AFTER your interaction, review your actions and ask yourself: Did I conduct myself with integrity, clarity, and respect? Did my presence leave others better off after dealing with me than they were before? Do I need to follow up on any misunderstandings, mistakes, or missed opportunities?

When you ask yourself these questions every day, you'll break the bad habit of focusing on "getting what I want" and allow yourself to envision the lifelong connections you want to build. You'll make things better while finding respectful ways to do it. You'll care about results, but you'll also care about what happens to others along the way. And the magical thing is when you invest time in the two "R"s of reputation and relationships, you'll achieve results that go far beyond anything you expected.

There's an old adage about two people who are laying bricks on a wall. One is mechanically going through the repetitive motions of spreading the mortar and putting the bricks in place. Asked what he's doing, he replies, "I'm laying bricks." The other person is performing the same actions, but with alacrity and a glow in his eye. When he's asked what he's doing, he says, "I'm building a cathedral."

When you create strong bonds that show other people that they're integral to your great outcome—and that you want to be a part of theirs—they won't just lay bricks for you. Together, you'll build cathedrals.

▶ *Usable Insight*

> *Every business transaction has its basis in a personal relationship.*
>
> David Bradford, former CEO of Fusion-IO

▶ *Action Step*

Look for opportunities to ask the other people involved in your conversations, meetings, or projects what would make it a great outcome for them. For example, ask:

- What would be the best use of your time in our conversation today?
- If this meeting (or project, initiative, presentation, etc.) goes as well as possible, what would be the outcomes?
- What would make this meeting a success for you?
- What would need to happen in our conversation to cause you to want to continue the conversation sooner?

STEP #2
Listen Past Your Blind Spot

To practice connected influence, you need to break down the barriers that keep you from knowing what other people really think, want, and need. In Section Three, you'll discover how to do that by "hearing the music" of other people's words, mastering the fourth level of listening, and being influenceable.

7

To Discover *Their There*, Listen to the Music

Listening is a magnetic and strange thing, a creative force.
The friends who listen to us are the ones we move toward.

Dr. Karl Menninger

Whatever your great outcomes are, you'll reach them only if you can connect with people. To do that, you need to get out of the blind spot that's keeping you trapped in **your here**. The very nature of a blind spot makes it difficult to see what's blocked by it. But when you can't see past your blind spot, you can listen past it.

In the sort of listening we're talking about—we call it *listening to learn*—there is an energetic, determined humility. Listening to learn implies we don't know already. It implies there is work to do in order to connect with people on their own terms, with as little distortion as possible from our own biases. It involves not surrendering our judgment, but suspending it.

When we master this type of listening, we draw others in and invite genuine buy-in. Listening with a strong personal motive to learn and understand more leads to real alignment and commitment, rather than creating resistance or the mere appearance of going along. This kind of listening is so potent that, as our next story shows, it can instantly change a relationship—or even change the world.

■ Ray Charles' Final Recording

Glen Barros is at the center of one of the most remarkable stories in the history of modern music.

Glen is the CEO of Concord Music Group, which focuses on what he calls "timeless music" that's not hit-driven or "here today, gone tomorrow." They have extensive back catalogues with classics in jazz, world music, blues, roots music, rock, pop, and R&B.

Concord also develops new recordings and looks for creative ways to reach their audience, and that's where this story begins. It's about making the legendary Ray Charles' final CD titled *Genius Loves Company*.

In 2003, Concord and Starbucks were discussing a partnership. At that point, Starbucks was selling music in their cafes, but the music they sold primarily consisted of existing recordings that were licensed from various record companies. Concord and Starbucks theorized that, with the millions of people coming through Starbucks cafes every day, they could co-create recordings that would reconnect artists who had become distanced from their fans. Glen said, "If you put a recording with a recognizable concept by a world-famous artist on the counter of every Starbucks store, you'll do customers, artists, and the world a great service."

Concord Music and Starbucks signed a deal, and then Concord set out to find the right project. Soon, the idea of approaching Ray

Charles for a duets album surfaced. Glen knew that this was the perfect project for the Starbucks venture: Ray was a household name and yet, at that point, near the end of his career, his new recordings hadn't been selling much.

A duets album, like the one Frank Sinatra had produced in the late 1980s, would be instantly recognizable and should be spectacular. Glen thought, "Who wouldn't want to sing with Ray Charles?" They could easily line up a list of prominent artists, young and old. And with Starbucks alongside, Ray's recent sales history didn't scare him; he knew that the visibility provided by Starbucks would make this project a success.

It was a brilliant idea—but it wasn't easy to get this extraordinary outcome off the ground.

Glen says it was difficult getting to a deal with Ray through his organization. His advisers were trying to protect his interests, but were making impossible requests. Luckily, Glen found a way to get through to Ray personally. He explained the roadblocks that made a deal unworkable and let him know that it looked as though the recording was not going to happen. Ray responded by saying, "Damn it, these people work for me! Get in here and I'll make the decisions!"

Glen sat down with Ray in Ray's office. At that point, he knew that his most important job was to find out why Ray and his advisers were being difficult. So instead of trying to sell Ray on the project, he simply *listened to learn*. And as he did, he found out why he'd had trouble getting through to Ray's team.

It turned out that people had taken advantage of Ray at different parts of his career. For example, money was recoupable out of the artist's earnings and in the past, every cost associated with the recording was recoupable, even the catering. Ray described how there would be big spreads laid out with steak, lobsters, wine—very expensive food and drink for other people to eat. It was all coming out of his pocket, and he wasn't even making those decisions.

Glen says, "In our meeting, Ray would say, 'I don't want to buy everyone's lunch!'"

Once he understood Ray's **there**, Glen had no trouble addressing his fears. He affirmed that that no one except for Ray would make any decisions about his money. Glen proposed a nontraditional business arrangement in which one side didn't benefit before the other. Ray said, "I see how that works; that's fair." The project was on.

The first track he recorded was with longtime friend and blues great, B.B. King. It had a playful feel to it—kidding around between old friends in the studio.

What no one knew at the time was that Ray was about to battle terminal cancer. Glen says, "Everything started off lighthearted, but after Ray realized where he was health-wise, you can hear it in the tracks. They took on a very different feel. He was making a profound and final statement."

The last track he recorded is the duet with Elton John. It almost didn't happen, because at that point Ray was so sick he wasn't able to make it into the studio. One morning he called John Burk, who was producing the record, and said, "I think I feel well enough, let's give it a shot." Elton, who happened to be recording his own record in Los Angeles and had known of Ray's condition, had said he'd drop everything whenever Ray was able.

Glen says, "It was a very moving session. It's something I'll never forget, seeing them in the studio together. I think Ray knew he had very little time left. Everyone was choked up. Elton John was so moved he had difficulty keeping it together, and the first rundown of the song didn't go well."

Sensing that others' concern for him was getting in the way, Ray—exhibiting both courage and his trademark charisma—tossed out a little friendly teasing to dispel the tension. He and Elton went back to work, and together, they laid down an extraordinary track. Even if it wasn't Ray's most technically perfect performance, the depth of feeling and the meaning that came through in his vocals were never more pronounced. It was the last song Ray Charles ever recorded.

Genius Loves Company went on to receive eight Grammy Awards, including Album of the Year, tying the most Grammys ever won by a single album. It also became Ray's most successful record ever, selling five-and-a-half million copies and counting. It led to something profoundly valuable for the artists, and for all of us who love music. And it wouldn't have happened without Glen's ability to listen.

Glen started with a great outcome in mind. To achieve it, he had to listen to learn in order to discover why Ray's advisers were impeding the deal, and why Ray himself distrusted music executives like Glen. He couldn't find the answers he needed using influence tactics or ploys. Instead, he needed to make an honest connection by truly hearing and understanding what Ray needed to say.

Once he did, the next steps—engaging Ray in **his there** and creating something even more amazing than they'd planned—became possible. And as a result, they made beautiful music together.

———

Listening in the way Glen did involves more than hearing. It's not just a matter of receiving information accurately and being able to repeat back to people what they said. And it's not merely a tedious mental chore: "I need to wait for this person to stop talking so I can make my point."

Instead, it's a fully involved experience. It's an immersion in understanding. It's looking, hearing, and feeling *into* another person's perspective, and learning from it.

Effective listening is an empathic exploration. It's an expedition into others' thoughts, feelings, mindsets, and attitudes. In effect, it's a journey to understanding.

What does it take to make this journey successfully? In Chapter

Eight, we'll show you how to master the actual steps of listening to learn (we like to call it "connective" listening). Like all of the steps of the connected influence model, this is a skill you can master mindfully.

But first, we'd like to talk just a little bit about the *music* of listening.

■ Learning to Listen from a Musician Who's Deaf

There is a wonderful presentation on TED.com titled "Evelyn Glennie shows how to listen." It's given by Scottish percussionist and composer Evelyn Glennie, who lost nearly all of her hearing as a young girl, yet went on to a groundbreaking career in music that's included winning two Grammys.

When somebody asks Glennie, "How do you hear?", she responds, "How do *you* hear? Is it only with your ears?" She says that she doesn't simply depend on her ears to hear music: "I also hear it through my hands, my arms, my cheekbones, my scalp, my tummy, my chest, my legs, and so on."

True listening, she says, isn't something that merely happens to you. It's something to do and to feel, to throw yourself into rationally, emotionally, and physically. Listening is something to engage with multiple senses. It isn't passive or reactive; it's creative. And to do it well, you must *feel* the experience—not just *think* about it.

Glennie's advice is as true when it comes to listening to people as it is for listening to music. Rather than analyzing someone's words disconnectedly—which will instinctively make you start thinking of objections, counterarguments, or excuses—you should listen to them as if you're listening to music. Experience the tone, tempo, rhythm, harmony, and emotion. Listen not just for the words being said, but for *how* the words are said, and (very important) for what's *not* being said. When we listen to each other, Glennie says, we should stop judging and instead "use our bodies as a resonating chamber."

Glennie also warns about the danger of demanding immediate "chemistry" when it comes to either music or human relationships. She notes that ninety-nine percent of the music she deals with is new, and "it's very easy for me to say, 'Oh yes, I like that piece. Oh no, I don't like that piece.'" But she adds, "You know, I just find that I have to give those pieces of music real time. It may be that the chemistry isn't quite right between myself and that particular piece of music, but that doesn't mean I have the right to say it's a bad piece of music." Similarly, she says, we need to take the time to "interpret" the people we meet in order to truly appreciate them.

And here's one more important point Glennie makes: There is no objectivity in listening. For instance, she notes that when you're listening to music, you may be above the instrument, below it, or in a different part of the concert hall. As a result, each person hears a different concert, even though they're all listening to the same performance.

In the same way, when it comes to interpersonal communication, we all bring our own thoughts, feelings, passions, hang-ups, biases, blind spots, abilities, ambitions, and experience into what we say and what we hear. That's why it's so important to respect the subjectivity in listening. We need to constantly remind ourselves that like the people in Glennie's concert audiences—or the tappers and listeners we talked about earlier—each person has a different experience in the same meeting, conversation, or speech. To truly understand and connect with others, we need to hear the music they hear and take time to appreciate it, even if it's not the melody we're hearing ourselves.

But listening to the music—breaking the habit of disconnected listening and instead listening to learn, just as Glen Barros did with Ray Charles—takes conscious work. To succeed, you'll need to actively unlearn the disconnected influence techniques you've learned, and replace them with "connective" skills that allow you to create true harmony. In Chapter Eight, we'll show you how to do this by practicing what we call level-four listening.

▶ *Usable Insight*
   To experience the music in other people's messages, listen from the "inside out" instead of from the "outside in."

▶ *Action Step*
   Over the next month, actively focus on listening to other people with your ears, eyes, heart, and body. For example:
   - Listen both to what they say and how they say it—their tone, pace, pitch, volume, variability, and rhythm. Also, in every important conversation you have, ask yourself: What is *not* being said?
   - Observe people's facial expressions and body language, and notice whether these match the words you're hearing.
   - Listen for people's moods and emotions. How do they feel about what they're saying? Why do you think they're saying it?
   - As you're listening, feel how their words resonate in your own body so you can mirror what they're experiencing. Ask yourself: What is it like for *them*? What is it like to *be* them? Listen to your "gut." Listen *with* your "gut."
   - Suspend your judgment before responding. Take time to listen, experience, understand, and try to understand more.

8

Master Level-Four Listening

Every person I work with knows something better than me.
My job is to listen long enough to find it and use it.
Jack Nichols, artist

We've compared listening to conversations with the act of listening to music, and the comparison runs even deeper. If you want to make great music, or to appreciate an opera or symphony with a trained ear, you need to develop your skills. And the same is true for connective listening. It doesn't just happen; you need to *make* it happen. Moreover, the more you practice, the better you'll become—and the better you become, the more remarkable your outcomes will be.

It may sound strange to practice listening. After all, you already listen to other people all day, every day. But here's the thing: There are different ways to listen, and not all of them work.

Disconnected influencers gravitate toward the least effective forms of listening, with the result that, as Mark Twain once said, "Most conversations are monologues in the presence of witnesses."

These types of conversations don't just make great outcomes difficult; they often bring them to a complete halt.

To practice the kind of connective listening that increases influence rather than destroying it, you need to train yourself to listen at a higher level. And to do that, you need to understand what happens at each level of listening.

Here are the four levels of listening, from worst to best.

■ Level One: Avoidance Listening = Listening *Over*

This is more the *avoidance* of listening than listening. Listeners who listen *over* others are the people who say, "Uh huh," while clearly showing no interest in what the other person is saying. They look preoccupied, and they usually are. Sometimes they don't even stop checking their e-mail or texting on their phones while they're "listening." The person who's talking usually feels ignored, blown off, or at the very least just not listened to. Level-one listening can annoy, exasperate, or even infuriate the person who's talking.

■ Level Two: Defensive Listening = Listening *At*

This is listening with your defenses up. It's being quick to react and slow to consider. Listeners who listen *at* others take issue with everything they're saying. Rather than taking things seriously, they take everything personally. Such listeners are often seen as high maintenance, and over time, people avoid them because they're exhausting. Level-two listening frustrates and upsets the people who are talking.

▣ Level Three: Problem-Solving Listening = Listening *To*

This is listening in order to accomplish things. It's problem-solving listening. It's a no-nonsense, purposeful exchange of information. Problem-solving listeners listen for the facts in order to move forward.

In the correct circumstances, this is the right approach. But people will feel frustrated if they're hoping for something more than a solution to a problem. Level-three listening can cause anxious people to calm down a little, but often it still leaves them feeling unsatisfied, unrelieved, and misunderstood.

When you're trying to get things done with people, a common mistake is to use problem-solving listening because it seems efficient. It focuses on the task at hand and drives toward results-oriented suggestions and recommendations. The problem is that it's a false efficiency. People aren't machines, waiting for information to be programmed into them so they can go about their tasks mechanistically. Level-three listening, especially when matters are complex or emotionally charged, leaves too much room for misunderstanding.

▣ Level Four: Connective Listening = Listening *Into*

This is listening of the highest order, and it's the human listening that all of us crave. Connective listeners strive to understand in the fullest sense. It's important for them to feel where people are coming from so they can establish genuine rapport.

When you're in connective listening, you're not acting as if listening is a burden and trying to avoid doing it (level 1); or listening with a mind-set to defend yourself against inaccuracies or perceived attacks (level 2); or listening in order to jump in with your solutions and quick fixes (level 3). Instead, you're listening with the intention to understand the other person and forge a stronger connection.

Connective listening is listening *into* other people to discover what's going on inside them. It's listening from **their there**, instead of **your here**. It's listening without an agenda, because you're not focused on responding or even on helping. That's because you can help more effectively later, when the time is right, if you don't prejudge what another person needs (which might be very different than you think).

As we discussed in Chapter Seven, connective listening involves listening fully—with your ears, eyes, heart, and body. In addition, it involves creating space to listen and being fully present. Here's how to do it.

THE ART OF LEVEL-FOUR LISTENING

1. Whenever possible, pick a time and place where the other person will feel comfortable being open with you.
2. Pause often, using silence to leave room for the person to think more and say more.
3. Eliminate distractions and give one hundred percent of your attention to the person you're listening to. Listen as if nothing more important is going on in the world than connecting with this person. Let the other person's words resonate within you.
4. Mindfully resist the urge to retreat into **your here** by offering solutions, defending yourself, or explaining yourself. Instead, remember that you are listening to learn. Ask questions like these:

What does that mean for you?
How do you feel about . . . ?
What do you think about . . . ?
What else comes to mind?
What else are you thinking/feeling?
What's your take on . . . ?
What's your perspective on . . . ?
What was your first reaction when you heard?
What's the best thing about that?
What would be the best way to build on that?
How can you keep the momentum continuing?

As you begin using level-four listening, understand that it isn't always easy. In fact, you're likely to find that it is by far the most challenging step of the connected influence model, and that it takes time and practice to get good at it.

To understand why, think back to the human nature traps we talked about in Chapter Two. Your brain is wired to be defensive (fight or flight), to believe that you're right, to fall into your habit handicaps, and to denigrate listeners who don't understand the message you're "tapping." So at first, you may struggle to avoid becoming defensive, judgmental, or quick fix–focused when you hear something like:

"Your plan won't work."
"I don't agree with you."
"You're wrong."
"I can't do what you want me to do."
"There's no solution for this problem."

But here's the good news: Each time you successfully handle conversations like these, it will get easier. (Think of this as developing your listening "muscles.") And as you observe the remarkable changes in how people respond to you, you'll be motivated to do it again and again.

In fact, if you're like our power influencers, you will actively seek experiences where you can practice level-four listening, because it will lead you to answers you can't find on your own. And often, those answers will lead to amazing results. Here's an example.

■ Creating Space to Listen

Calvin Abe is the president of ABHE Landscape Architecture, a firm that does award-winning work in landscape design, urban design, and environmental planning.

Calvin is passionate about his great outcome: reconnecting city and nature. "The premise of this place," he says, "is to create a space where the enterprise can contribute to the planet. There's no other reason for being here. It's a stand we take." And he's equally passionate about listening to the people who are helping him translate this dream into a reality.

He says, "Listening leads me to rediscover my own integrity. People call me on it. Someone might say, 'You talk about collaboration, but I'm not getting it from you.' I have people around me who will call me on my nonsense. That's so empowering for me."

"Creating space" is a core theme for how Calvin sees his role as leader of the organization. As the leader, he says, he needs to create space for his designers to do their work, to constructively handle conflict with one another, and to learn and grow as professionals.

The space that Calvin constantly strives to create enables listening to occur. And frequently, he's the one doing most of the listening.

He says, "How do you create the space for conflict to be about commitment rather than a contest? It's not a method, it's a dance, you don't really think about it. It's about letting people step into their conflict, and listening without judgment or redirection. It's about hearing their issue and not reacting to the issue, feeding into the frenzy. Most people want to be heard, to have their feelings expressed. If you know that, you listen, and when you strive to set an example by listening to people, they tend to find their own solutions."

Recently the firm faced a challenge when they needed to significantly increase staff hours but lacked the resources. It was placing stress on the organization, and everyone knew it. Calvin called a meeting, wrote the projects and schedules on a whiteboard, and sat down. He said nothing. He listened. It was up to the team.

Discussion began, and eventually, one of the junior project managers proposed a creative way of distributing staff hours that accomplished the most important priorities. "No one got exactly what they wanted," said Calvin, "but everyone came out okay."

When Calvin is leading, even when he doesn't say a word, there's always more at stake than the immediate agenda items. "Coming out okay" isn't just about the task at hand; it's about continuing to improve and develop and look for ways to make things better.

"This place is a life laboratory," says Calvin. "It's a place to grow as a human being."

■ Allowing People to "Exhale"

Level-four listening is effective not just because it gets results, but because—as Calvin notes—it helps people to grow as human beings. It transforms conflicts into fertile ground where new ideas can take root. It lets everyone contribute to making things better, no matter what their role is in an organization.

And level-four listening accomplishes an additional miracle: It allows people to "exhale."

In today's world, it's easy to get overloaded when we're dealing with difficult people at work, crises at home, a deluge of e-mail and text, honking horns on the freeway, and upsetting news on the radio, Internet, and television. As a result, we're like overloaded modems. Our capacity to absorb information or understand other people is maxed out, and nothing is going to get through to us.

When a modem gets overloaded and can no longer conduct information between the Internet and your computer, what are you instructed to do? Disconnect it, let it rest and have all the memory drain out, and then reboot it.

It's the same with people. When you listen not just to what they're saying, but what they mean to say—and even more deeply, to what they're feeling—you allow them to disconnect and release the tension, stress, anger, fear, or disappointment they're holding inside. When you do this, they in turn become able to listen to *you*.

When people are especially stressed or overwhelmed, one particular approach can help you "unplug the modem." If you've read Mark's book, *Just Listen*, you've already learned this method for allowing people to exhale. If not, here's how to do it.

When people who are upset or angry vent their feelings, they expect you to come back at them, become defensive, give unsolicited advice, or just run away. Instead, you should do the last thing they expect: Encourage them to say more. To do this, use conversation deepeners like these:

■ "Say more about _____" (selecting words or phrases that have some emotional energy to them, as if you're picking a scab and letting the pus underneath drain).
■ "Really . . . " (said as if you're saying, "You don't say . . . ," which will encourage them to continue).
■ "And so . . . " (helping them focus on the message they're trying to send).

When you do this, you actually *see* people exhale in response. As they vent their frustration or anger or fear, their shoulders drop, their facial expression changes, and their breathing becomes relaxed. What's more, they're grateful for the burden you lifted from them, and they're likely to respond by wanting to help you in return.

Of course, not all people are in a place where they need to exhale (although most of us feel this way at least part of the time). But even when people aren't feeling anxious or upset, level-four listening can bring out the best in them. It can inspire people, help them think outside the box, and motivate them to give deep thought to the important issues in their lives.

> Rabbi Nachum Braverman is based in Los Angeles, and (among many activities) runs a men's group that Mark has attended for several years. He has a powerful reputation for helping people think about their lives and find the wisdom to make good choices.
>
> Rabbi Braverman's approach to listening reflects the method of Socrates, who would invite people into easy conversation and then help them move toward more meaningful reflections.
>
> Socrates might say something like, "I see you're very busy and rushing around with lots of things to do—you must have thought much about what's important in life." In a similar way, Rabbi Braverman asks simple questions—What did you eat? Where did you go?—and then leads people gently into more personal and substantial issues: Do you like the work you do? Are you happy with your life? Why or why not? He invites people to talk about who they are, what they're doing, and why they made the choices they did. Following up leads to deeper discussions about their goals, their families, living well, and dying well.
>
> Rabbi Braverman says, "My only goal is to be helpful, to

genuinely care about people, and be worthy of their trust. I care, and I try to understand. I think about their lives in the same way I think about my children's lives. I think that helps them open up."

He adds, "I listen more than talk. People typically don't listen very carefully to others. They don't try to understand and clarify what others want to say and help them articulate it. Instead, most people listen with the hope of getting something from the other person, or they turn around promptly and give their own views without trying to understand what the person just said."

He observes, "Most people don't have that kind of experience of being listened to, *ever*. Most men in particular don't have a community of men in which they can talk frankly about things. Many men are lonely because they don't have that kind of listening."

As Rabbi Braverman's work shows, connective listening can help you wield positive influence in your personal life as well as your professional life. Similarly, as a psychiatrist who's counseled thousands of individuals and families, Mark has found that in nearly every case, the first step in influencing people to change their lives for the better is high-level listening. This simple act can create insight, ease emotional pain, and often even allow you to connect with people who've been angry, antagonistic, or apathetic for years.

To practice this type of healing listening with the people closest to you, Mark says, you need to set aside your own grievances, agenda, and ego. Then, ask about what's *really* going on underneath. For instance, in the middle of a heated argument, simply stop and say, "So tell me, what's really going on for you?" If the person vents, don't attack or defend yourself. Simply listen to learn. When you show the people in your life that you care enough to listen to them in this way, they will relax and open their minds to you rather than throwing up barricades to keep you out.

One influencer we spoke with, prominent venture capitalist and entrepreneur Brad Feld, shared his own story about using level-four listening to save the most important relationship in his life: the one with his wife. Currently, Brad is managing director of the Foundry Group, a venture capital firm. He's also a cofounder of TechStars, a leading start-up accelerator organization. Brad told us that he learned from experience about the toll that the pressure of a career can take. Early in his own career, it nearly cost him his marriage.

In 2001, during a period of extraordinary intensity and after a particularly stressful week when as usual he was focused almost entirely on work, his wife Amy said very quietly, "I'm done."

Brad said, "Yeah, it's been a tough week"

Amy said, "No you don't get it. You're not even a good roommate anymore."

He needed to listen, and he knew it. So he said, "Tell me what to do. Give me some rules."

Amy said, "That doesn't sound very romantic." Brad noted that she was right. It wasn't the most romantic gesture he could have made, but it wasn't about gestures anymore. He needed to change, and he needed to listen in order to succeed. He told her, "Give me some guidelines and you'll see; I can do it. But I'm missing it—tell me what I need to hear."

So she did. And he listened.

As a result of that conversation, they now take regular breaks together, and he goes "off the grid." During these times he gives her his cell phone, and at his own request she doesn't give it back until their break is over.

Amy also told him they needed to go out together for a relaxing, special dinner once a month. They would give each other a little gift and make a celebration out of the first day of every month.

Brad said, "I don't know if I can do that one."

Amy said, "You have a calendar on your computer, right?"

"Yes."

"Then make an appointment on your calendar for the first day of next month, and make it recurring. Until forever."

So that's what he did.

Brad's ability to listen to his wife saved his marriage that day. He didn't do what most husbands would do in this situation: ignore his wife (level one), lash out viciously or try to defend himself (level two), or go for the quick fix by saying something like, "Fine, I'll take you out to dinner next week and we'll spend some time together" (level three). Instead, he went to **her there** and made the effort to find out what it was like for her.

As a result, they were able to restore the deep bond they'd had earlier in their lives. They recreated a relationship that Brad says is "a safe place to start from, and a safe place to return when things get hard." And the experience also led to a surprising great outcome: a website, life.startuprev.com, where Brad and his wife offer relationship advice for entrepreneurs.

■ Practicing Level-Four Listening . . . with *Everyone*

Just as level-four listening can create relationships that lead to great outcomes, it can take corporations to new heights of achievement. Frequently, Mark and John have sparked amazing turnarounds in once-failing companies simply by teaching CEOs and managers the skill of level-four listening.

But in a corporate setting, just learning to listen isn't enough. It's also crucial to listen to *everyone*—not just VIPs or upper managers. In addition to practicing higher-level listening techniques, the influencers we've interviewed make it a point to listen to all the people they come in contact with professionally.

For example, Dave Vucina, the former CEO of Wayport

Wireless—the firm that invented the concept of Wi-Fi hotspots in cafes, hotels, airports, and restaurants—turned a failing company into a success largely by making it a point to hear what everyone in his company had to say.

When Dave took over as CEO in 2001, the company was on the verge of shutting down. But a few years later, when the company was sold at a premium, it was on multiple "Best Companies to Work For" lists, and AT&T named it one of their top fifty vendors out of over five thousand.

What sparked this dramatic turnaround? One huge factor was connective listening, practiced in large ways and small.

When Dave took over, he made it a priority to listen to employees, customers, vendors, stakeholders . . . everyone. For example, one group of employees raised a question about how much the company was spending on free sodas for employees. It turned out to be $180,000 per year. They asked, "Is this the best use of the company's money? How about spending those funds on hiring people or giving raises to excellent performers, or for research and development?" The employees took a vote, and seventy-eight percent of the employees opted to get rid of the free soda.

Dave could easily have made a top-down decision to cut costs by eliminating free sodas—the route most CEOs would choose. Instead, he listened to what mattered to his employees.

A much bigger decision had to do not with cutting costs, but raising revenue. Wayport wanted to expand into retail venues such as McDonald's, Starbucks, and Barnes & Noble. The board of directors pushed back, saying the revenue models were suspect. And how could they beat bigger providers like T-Mobile and British Telecom?

It was a great question. How *could* they compete against the largest providers with all their advantages and win a major account like McDonald's? Wayport's network speed was comparable to the competition, but the major providers could play to Wayport's weaknesses by offering free equipment and the advantage of being associated with their brands.

Dave didn't have an answer. But he'd created a culture where both he and his managers listened to all of their employees, and it paid off.

During a break in one team meeting, an employee offered this insight: It's not about our routers and equipment; it's about how we can help McDonald's sell more hamburgers.

The idea ignited the team and refocused their attention on how to do that. They shifted their attention from Wayport's **here** (their equipment and internet service) to McDonalds' **there** (selling hamburgers). And they came up with a breakthrough idea. They'd say to Verizon, Sprint, and AT&T: "Tell your customers, if you're on the road and you need the Internet, just stop into a McDonalds."

Wayport created a revenue-sharing arrangement that was much more attractive for users than the prevailing model at the time. They sold to businesses instead of individuals, making Wi-Fi easier, cheaper, and more accessible. And everyone gained.

From the telecoms, Wayport went on to strategic partners. They went to Nintendo because they had a game system with a Wi-Fi chip enabling users to play games with people around the world. Wayport suggested they tell users, "When you want to game on the road . . . stop at McDonald's." It worked for everyone: Nintendo's users had more mobility; Nintendo attracted more customers; McDonald's increased their business; and, of course, Wayport made money.

They won the McDonald's account and many others over their larger, better funded, more strongly branded competitors. McDonald's was so impressed that they offered to invest in Wayport, to make sure it would never go away as a service provider.

Dave says, "I've learned more from employees than from any single person. I've been around fantastic leaders, but I've learned more from employees. I tell people instead of focusing primarily on senior people, reverse direction and talk to as many people as you can inside and outside your organization. Interact with lots of people who know lots of things and listen for things you don't know."

———

We can't think of a better definition than Dave's for the art of connective listening. Whether you're listening to your coworkers, your clients, your friends, or your family members, begin by assuming that they have something of value to tell you. Set aside your ego and your agenda, and resist the urge to defend, argue, or explain. And then simply *listen for things you don't know.*

Because here's a secret. No matter how much you think you know about other people—even your partner, your child, or someone who's worked one desk over from you for twenty years—those people will surprise you if you make space for them to tell you what they really know and feel. And the information you find out can point the way to deeper understanding, creative solutions, and huge wins for everyone.

▶ *Usable Insight*

Think about how your listening behavior will change if you commit yourself to sending the message: "I care about you. I care about what's important to you."

▶ *Action Steps*

1. Use level-four listening at least once a day over the next week with a variety of people. Remember that you aren't pushing an agenda, being defensive, trying to get your way, or demonstrating your intelligence. You are simply trying to hear the other people fully and accurately, and giving them more space to identify and articulate their feelings.

2. Just as Calvin Abe did, try stating a challenge, issue, need, or problem, and then create the room and opportunity for others to step in and fill the space.

3. Listen with purpose, but leave your agenda at the door. Famous psychoanalyst Wilfred Bion said, "The purest form of listening is to listen without memory or desire." When you listen with memory, you have an old agenda; when you listen with desire, you have a new agenda that you're trying to plug the other person in. But in neither case are you listening for *their there*. Make it your purpose to do so.

9

To Influence,
Be Influenceable

In the perspective of every person lies a lens
through which we may better
understand ourselves.

Ellen J. Langer, psychology professor

In our careers, the two of us work with a wide variety of people, from corporate CEOs to families. No matter who we're helping, we find that people immediately sense the value of level-four listening. They want to do it. They're committed to transforming their conversations from monologues or shouting matches to learning experiences.

But sometimes they find it really, really hard.

Why? One reason, as we said in Chapter Eight, is that level-four listening is a learned skill. It takes time to break old habits and get good at it.

And there's another reason we mentioned earlier—the human nature traps that are always waiting to trip you up. These traps keep you in **your here**, rather than letting you go to **their there**.

If you're having trouble achieving level-four listening and find yourself sliding back into arguing or defending or avoiding, you'll need to work at overcoming these human nature traps by being sure you fully accept a new philosophy well *before* you go into a conversation.

That philosophy is: To influence, be influenceable.

Being influenceable isn't about giving in, giving up, being weak or soft, being scared, or being any less committed to your principles and to achieving excellent results. And being influenceable doesn't mean that you're not going to disagree.

What being influenceable *does* mean is that you go into every conversation being willing to believe that you may be partially or totally wrong; that the other person may be partially or completely right; and that even if the other person isn't right, you will learn something valuable from your interaction.

Being influenceable means being both open-minded and open-hearted. People tend to open their minds to people who've opened their own minds, and to open their hearts to people who permit themselves to be touched. When you want to strengthen your influence with others who see things differently, being vulnerable is more potent than being impervious.

However, being influenceable is harder than it seems, especially when (1) you have good intentions; (2) you're trying to do the right thing; and (3) you've done your homework. In this situation, you feel confident about your point of view, you feel strongly about your positive motives, and you anticipate the helpful results that will come from following your approach. So you're totally focused on influencing—not on being influenced.

You're also especially likely to have a hard time being open-minded when you're in high-stress situations. That's because when you feel very stressed or pressured, it's easy to personalize your influence problems. For instance, you're likely to think:

"That person isn't listening to me."

"Those people don't see the value I have to offer."

"That person is getting in my way."

"Those people are undermining me."

When you believe that the problem resides in another person or group, you'll find yourself focusing on trying to change that person or group. For instance, you'll think:

"I need to get him to listen to me."

"I need to get them to see the value I have to offer."

"I need to get her out of my way."

"I need to prevent them from undermining me."

If you come at people from this direction, you risk being perceived as closed-minded and emotionally self-indulgent. You think you're being helpful, honest, and true, but instead you'll be seen as self-serving and self-centered.

To see why, try thinking of it from the other side of the interaction. What's it like when someone tries to influence you as if they have the answers, and as if you should simply do what they want you to do? For instance . . .

- Do you like it when others presume *they're* logical and you're not?
- Do you like it when others presume *they're* rational and you're not?
- Do you like it when others presume *they're* right and you're not?

Of course you don't. And other people don't like it if you do it to them.

If you aren't seen as influenceable when different points of view arise, you lose credibility and connection. You appear preprogrammed to reject other people's ideas and follow a self-advantageous path to your preferred outcome. And worst of all, as our next story shows, you risk making very bad decisions.

■ Night Falls on Nike Town . . . Almost

Marilyn Tam has a power résumé that includes serving as CEO of Aveda and president of Reebok Apparel and Retail Group. But one of her favorite stories about influence comes from the early days of her career, in the late 1980s.

Back then, Marilyn was running one of the divisions for a regional apparel chain. Someone suggested that she should talk with a guy from Oregon who wanted to grow a chain of specialty stores. It was Phil Knight, CEO of Nike.

Marilyn was excited about the opportunity to create a whole new store concept. Until then, she'd been working with existing stores. Here was her chance to shape things from the beginning.

But when she looked into Nike's products, she knew there was a problem. They were riding on the enormous popularity of their shoes, which were designed and manufactured to high-quality standards. That wasn't the case, however, for their clothing and other accessories. In fact, it seemed to Marilyn that Nike was simply ordering inexpensive stock items, putting a Nike label on them, and pricing them at a premium.

Marilyn knew this would damage the company's reputation and had the potential to cause a host of other business problems. As she prepared for her meeting with Phil Knight, Marilyn considered the four principles that she lives by at work:

1. Tell the truth.
2. Make partners.

3. Make big mistakes.
4. Die by your own sword.

She could see that her meeting with Knight would be a challenge. If she told the truth, it could make for an uncomfortable first (and possibly last) meeting. Rather than becoming partners with Knight, she had a good chance of achieving two of her other principles—making a big mistake and dying by her own sword—all in one meeting.

Marilyn flew to Oregon, and the interview went exceedingly well. So well, in fact, that Knight offered her the job on the spot. She replied, "As much as I would like to work with you, if you open a store right now, you will fail."

Knight was not pleased. As Marilyn said to us, "It ended the conversation quickly."

She flew home, feeling that she'd given up a great opportunity but at least had held to her principles. Then, a few weeks later, the phone rang. It was Phil Knight.

He told her, "I thought about what you said, and I did some research. You're right. Instead of opening the stores now, you figure out the apparel and accessories that are up to the standards and reputation of Nike in the marketplace."

So she did. And in the process, she helped transform apparel and accessories from "also-rans" into key elements that enhanced Nike's image and success.

Better late than too late, Phil Knight became influenceable, and night didn't fall on Nike Town.

▪ The Fatal Concept of Winning and Losing

Phil Knight's very wise decision saved Nike from making a mistake that could have killed his store chain. And there are countless other scenarios in which being influenceable, rather than insisting on being right, will stop you from making fatal mistakes.

One way to avoid making these mistakes is to catch yourself when you hear your inner voice gloating, "I'm winning this argument" or warning, "I'm losing this argument." Here's the all-important rule to remember in these situations: *To strengthen your interpersonal influence, don't win arguments. Instead, win hearts and minds.*

Trying to win arguments implies that you *are* arguing, and this is a recipe for failure. When you argue, you trigger people's urge to defend themselves or incite their natural instinct to prevail over you. Quickly, the situation becomes more about winning or losing—and when that happens, your passion and preparation actually undermine your progress. ("He just made a strong point. I'd better come back with one that hits him in the gut.") When ego trumps substance, you're destined to lose sooner or later.

And while you think you're coming across as strong and forceful in an argument, you're not. If you don't demonstrate intellectual and emotional openness, you risk being seen as a zealot or an autocrat or a fool. Come across as closed-minded, and people mentally put you into a box, close it, and stamp it with a label: "Disregard."

Be aware, too, that subtler forms of arguing can trip you up. Often, for instance, we hear managers justifying a closed-minded attitude because they're "sticking up for their people." The flaw in this argument is that if they're sticking up for their people by refusing to consider the viewpoints of other people, they're framing conversations as win-lose situations—and that means everyone loses.

> Karl was the European theater lead for informational technology in a global technology firm. The company's headquarters and the vast majority of executives and employees were located in the United States. That's where the power was, where the most

influential people were, and where priorities and resources were focused.

The outlying theaters tended to be left with leftovers, so Karl thought he was doing the right thing when he weighed in vigorously in defense of his region's interests and priorities. They were the underdogs. They lacked a strong voice. They needed a champion.

Karl felt that if he didn't strongly advocate for the interests of his region, no one else would. If he didn't stand up for his people, he reasoned, the European part of the business would suffer from neglect. That would hurt prospects for the organization, which needed to expand into overseas markets. Karl didn't want to disappoint the people who were counting on him.

Over time, however, a gap steadily grew between Karl's self-perception as a good-for-the-company regional advocate and the way others perceived him. Nobody brought it directly to Karl's attention until one day Karl asked one of his peers, Michelle, for help on an initiative. In a rare moment of political incorrectness for this team, Michelle looked him straight in the eyes and said, "No Karl. I don't want to help you."

"What?" Karl said, reeling. "Why not?"

Michelle paused a moment, looking at him as if deciding whether to be honest or play it safe. In the end, honesty won out. "Why not? Because you're a pain in the ass to work with, that's why not."

"What do you mean?" Karl asked, confused.

Michelle went on. "You want my help? I bet you do. Every issue, every time, it's all about *your* theater, *your* people, what *you* need, and what *you* want. It's tiresome. You're not a team player. You never change your tune. You're always trying to get more for your region, so you can look better. Well I don't care if you look better anymore."

Karl was stunned. "But I don't want . . . " he started to say.

Michelle interrupted him. "Frankly, I'm tired of hearing what you want and don't want. That's the problem. It's always about you."

Karl opened his mouth, but he didn't know what to say. He was in shock. Michelle walked away.

For Karl, this conversation was a bolt out of the blue. He prided himself on being an ethical, dedicated, hardworking professional. He wasn't out for himself; he was trying to do the right thing. To him, it seemed like Michelle's comments were about an entirely different person.

"Is it just Michelle?" he thought. "Maybe she's the problem."

Luckily, Karl wasn't totally incapable of being influenceable. So he reached out to other peers and had one-to-one discussions with them, emphasizing how important it was for him to hear the truth about how they perceived him.

The results stunned him: They all agreed with Michelle. They had different ways of saying it, and some were more hesitant than others, but there it was. The evidence was overwhelming.

Karl had thought he was open-minded, but it didn't matter what he thought. To others, he wasn't. Despite his good intentions, he came across as selfish and even careerist. Without realizing it, he'd strained key working relationships and harmed his reputation, and it took an enormous amount of time and hard work for him to repair the damage.

As Karl discovered, when people think you're not open to listening, they're not motivated to listen. Come across as closed-minded, and you're like the teacher in the *Charlie Brown* cartoons. Whatever the teacher says, all the kids hear is "blah blah blah." Say anything you want—logically, persuasively, passionately, or poetically. If you say it with a closed mind, it all gets the same translation: "Blah, blah, blah."

When you're influenceable, however, it's possible to get buy-in for your ideas even if you think or feel very differently than another person does. That's because you'll lean into each other, rather than resisting each other. And when that happens, you'll nearly always be able to find common ground.

To fully demonstrate to other people that you're influenceable, you'll need to practice the following two types of openness.

Intellectual openness: This means being open to other people's logic, data, analysis, and ideas. In addition, it means genuinely taking an interest in how others think, and acknowledging how their ideas are influencing you. Intellectually open influencers say things like:

- "You've really changed my thinking on this."
- "I haven't thought about it that way before."
- "Help me understand how you're thinking through this. I want to make sure I'm following you."
- "I think you can help me open my perspective a bit more on this."
- "Ah, it sounds like you see it differently. Tell me more."
- "I was wrong."
- "You're right!"

Emotional openness: This means being open to other people's feelings, passions, values, drives, motives, beliefs, and convictions. When you practice emotional openness, you'll actively work to understand what other people are experiencing and why they feel the way they do. Emotionally open influencers say thing like:

- "How are you feeling about the situation?"
- "What's at stake for you here?"
- "What's most important for you about this issue?"
- "What does your experience tell you about the position we're in?"

But openness isn't the only skill you need to develop. In addition to practicing intellectual and emotional openness, you need to master one additional—and essential—skill. Think of it as the art of "shutting up."

The next time someone's speaking with you and you feel yourself becoming angry or defensive, *do not say the next thing you want to say—no matter how much you want to say it*. Instead, stop and ask yourself: "Why am I pushing back at what this person is saying?"

Then ask yourself: "Is it what he's saying? If so, what specifically am I disagreeing with? Or is it how he's saying it to me?"

Either way, take a deep breath and ask the person: "What is the most important point you need me to understand, and why is it important from your point of view?" This will allow you to shift back into level-four listening, so you can fully understand what the other person is telling you.

When this happens, you might not hear anything useful. You might indeed find that the person truly doesn't have anything worthwhile to say.

Or, like Phil Knight, you might get a message that will save you from making one of the biggest mistakes of your life.

▶ *Usable Insight*
Don't triumph over others; triumph with them.

▶ *Action Steps*
1. If you're a team leader or manager, think of the people around you who are intelligent, creative, and passionate, and who may have much more to contribute than you are allowing them. If you don't know who these people are, ask others in your organization to point them out.

2. Set up an appointment to meet with these people and say to them: "I'm told that you have some great ideas, and I've never

given you the opportunity to share them with me. I'm all ears now. How do you think we can do better?"

3. Think about an issue that's causing a rift between you and your life partner, or you and your child. Ask your partner or child to offer his or her perspective about the issue—and as you listen, commit yourself to being influenceable rather than influencing. In particular, remember to exhibit emotional openness; to exhibit intellectual openness; and, above all, to avoid saying the next thing you want to say, and instead simply listen.

STEP #3
Engage Them in *Their There*

Once you understand where other people are coming from, it's time to connect with them in a way that makes them want to support you. To do this, you need to practice the "three gets of engage." In addition, you need be willing to be provocative, to take some big risks, and to break down barriers in creative ways.

10

Use the Three
Gets of Engage

When you start treating people like people,
they become people.
Paul Vitale, author

When you really listen to people, you'll find out where they're coming from. And once that happens, you're ready for the next step in real influence: engaging these people in *their there*.

To understand why this step is so important, imagine that you're at one end of a shopping mall—say, the northeast corner, over by Starbucks. Next, imagine that a friend of yours is at the opposite end of the mall, next to the toy store. And imagine that you're telling that person how to get to where you are.

Now, picture yourself saying, "To get to where I am, start in the northeast corner by Starbucks." That doesn't make any sense, does it? Because that's where *you* are, not where the other person is.

Yet that's how you're trying to connect with people if you're using a disconnected influence model. You're coming from your own *here* and expecting the other person to start there, too. And that's not going to happen.

So to engage people fully, it's critical to do something very different from what disconnected influencers do. Once you've used level four listening to find out where another person is coming from, your goal is to approach things from that person's perspective. When you do this, it becomes exponentially easier for the person to connect with you.

The secret to reaching people in **their there** is to use what we call the "three gets of engage." By keeping these three "gets" in focus, you'll be able to shift quickly and effectively from your own perspective to another person's. Here's a look at them.

■ Situational Awareness: You Get "It"

In this get, you show that you understand the opportunities and challenges a person is facing. You grasp the person's reality in a way that rings true, and you offer ideas that work in the person's **there**. When you do this, you'll hear comments like "You really get it!" or "You really understand what I'm dealing with here."

For instance, in our example in Chapter One, Giselle Chapman showed her interviewer that she understood where he was coming from. He needed people who could get in to see doctors, and he needed to know what those doctors wanted. So she told him exactly what he needed to know—and she got the job.

Similarly, our "party crasher," Giang Biscan, started from the **there** of people hosting start-up events. Those people needed free or inexpensive publicity, clever ideas, and a helping hand—and Giang offered all of these. As a result, she now has start-ups and investors coming to her in droves.

■ Personal Awareness: You Get "Them"

In this get, you show that you understand other people's strengths, weaknesses, goals, hopes, priorities, needs, limitations, fears, and concerns. In addition, you demonstrate that you're willing to connect with them on a personal level. When you do this right, you'll hear people say things like "You really get me!" or "You really understand where I'm coming from on this."

One of our favorite examples involves Mike Critelli, former CEO of the extraordinarily successful company, Pitney Bowes. One of Mike's many strengths was the ability to motivate his staff to achieve high levels of performance. When we asked him about this, he said, "Very often what motivates people are the little gestures, and a leader needs to listen for those. It's usually not about negotiating salary down to the nickel. It's about picking up on other things that are most meaningful to people."

For example, one employee had a passing conversation with Mike about the challenges of adopting a child, pointing out that Pitney Bowes had an inadequate adoption benefit. A few weeks after that, he and his wife received a letter from Mike congratulating them on their new child—along with a check for the amount of the enhanced adoption benefit the company had just started offering.

■ Solution Awareness: You Get Their Path to Progress

We often speak about the need for leaders to "*en*spire" their people. Motivating people pumps them up, but they often deflate back to their usual limiting beliefs and actions after the motivator leaves. Inspiring people lifts them up, but often leaves them not knowing what to do next. *En*spiring lifts people up, but also points them toward a great possibility that goes beyond a mere opportunity. When you get people's path to progress, you help them to reach places they never thought they'd reach.

In this get, you show people a positive path that enables them to make progress on their own terms. You give them options and alternatives that empower them. Based on your understanding of their situation and what's at stake for them personally, you show them possibilities for making things better—and you help them think more clearly, feel better, and act smarter. When you succeed, you'll hear comments like, "I see how that would help me."

This is one of the key reasons why Glen Barros succeeded so spectacularly with Ray Charles. He saw that Ray had been burned by previous producers, and he identified a perfect solution: setting up a financial arrangement that made it impossible for anyone to take advantage of Ray. This showed Ray that Glen wasn't in it just for the money—he was also in it for Ray, for the other performers, and for the music.

When you practice all three of these gets—situational, personal, and solution-oriented—you understand who people are, what they're facing, and what they need in order to move forward. Consistently, the three gets will take you to people's **their there** and then help you get them to where they want to be and could be. This is a powerful way to achieve great outcomes—and as one of our influencers shows, it's also a great way to transform a very bad scenario into a win-win situation.

■ Turning an Angry Mob into an Appreciative Audience

We introduced you in Chapter Six to Joey Gold, a rock musician turned aerospace engineer. Joey has countless stories of keeping things together on the road with his band, Love/Hate—especially when they toured Europe with Ozzy Osbourne.

As traveling companions, Joey and his band had to fully get where Ozzy and his wife, Sharon, were coming from—not just musically, but personally—in order to keep things on track. For instance, Joey says that at the beginning of the tour, "we were told by Sharon Osbourne that Ozzy was sober and under no circumstances were we to have alcohol in our dressing rooms or on stage for the tour. The stakes were high so we complied. Sure enough, on the third day of the tour, the 'Prince of Darkness' himself, Ozzy, comes in our dressing room to say hello, acting nonchalant. Within a minute he asks if we have a beer. We say no. He calls us liars and immediately dumps our ice chest upside down looking for anything with some alcohol in it. Finding nothing, he moves on and wishes us a good show."

But staying on the good side of the infamously temperamental Ozzie and his fiery wife wasn't the only challenge Joey dealt with during his rock star days. Other crises involved his own band members. In one case in particular, he had to use the three gets of engaging to turn an utter disaster into a huge success.

It happened when he and the band sold out two large venues in London, and the record company asked them to do a big "in-store" (where band members autograph records, jackets, CDs, and other items for fans). The location was famed Tower Records Piccadilly London, which announced that the band would play an acoustic set of four songs on a ministage the store built for the occasion.

"Before we leave the hotel though," Joey says, "we get in a massive fight. I can't remember it all now but it was something about the bass player (and writer) wanting to play acoustic guitar at the in-store and not wanting the guitarist to play. We finally left in separate cars, because the egos, in retrospect—mine as well—were too big for one. The guys didn't bring their guitars because they refused to play."

Joey says, "We arrive and the manager of Tower Records is freaking out that we won't play. So are our Columbia Records reps. The crowd is getting unruly. Finally I say if we're not going to play, someone had better tell this crowd because it's hot, crowded, and the mood is getting dark because they sense something is up. They say, 'Fine, you do it.'"

Now, picture the challenge of engaging this crowd. They're big fans of the band, but right now, they're restless and angry. They've come to hear a popular band play live music, and they aren't getting what they want.

So Joey understands who they are, what their situation is, and what needs to happen in order to solve their problem. And he engages them on all three levels.

He walks out alone onto the stage and grabs a microphone. "I tell them we're not playing. Boos ring out. I try to quiet them and ask if they want to know the reason why. They already know the reason—they expect a lame excuse such as that the singer has laryngitis. Everyone always cancels for that reason even though everyone knows it's nonsense. Somebody must be drunk, hung over, or on drugs."

Joey doesn't make something up; he doesn't give his band members an "out." He looks for another way to address the issue. It's not about tending to his band members' egos; it's about engaging with the people who came to see them.

Joey says, "I give them the brutally honest truth. I tell them we're not playing because everyone's ego is so big that we got in a fight over who was going to be playing guitar and to make a point, they left their guitars at the hotel. Silence. The crowd is miffed and confused. I then hear a couple chuckles and decide to mine that vein a little more. I tell the crowd about the fight we got into the night before over something truly monumental—whether the jumbo prawns on our deli tray backstage at the show were indeed jumbo.

The crowd starts cracking up. I give them more—I launch into a torrent of embarrassing episodes from our offstage lives which make us all, myself included, look like total idiots. The crowd is now in hysterics. If they're not going to get a concert, this is what they want to hear—the truth."

Then he engages them by offering something that more than makes up for the lack of music. He tells the crowd, "We're only supposed to stay here two hours, but we'll stay here as long as you want, signing things, whatever you want. We're here for you."

Joey says, "The band was irate when I got off the stage for airing our dirty laundry. But I told them 'too bad, we all need to get out there and start signing.' We were there for over six hours. It was phenomenal. The band agreed it was one of the most worthwhile experiences we ever had, and we didn't even perform. We were talking with the fans in depth, not just signing and moving on, but engaging them, talking with them, and learning about them."

In short, Joey didn't try to talk his way out of the problem. He talked his way further *into* it. In doing so, he practiced *situational awareness* (these people are hot, tired, frustrated, and disappointed), *personal awareness* (they're our fans and they know they deserve better), and *solution awareness* (we need to give them something of value to make this encounter worth their while).

Joey says, "If we're taught in driver's education to turn into the skid when we drive, why not turn into the skid in other situations? Why not embrace the calamity and steer it to where you want to go? Why confront the energy of the crowd head on? Why not redirect it? Why not turn into the skid?"

Joey says the same strategy that worked that day in Tower Records also works in his current job in the aerospace industry. "A lot of what I do now is the same as the music business. I put together teams, I have a product line that I need to upkeep and sell, I negotiate licensing deals, I do damage control for temperamental people,

I handle money—it's all sort of the same. I'm just taking what I learned from the music industry and applying it to the aerospace industry. And let me tell you, some people think the music industry is supposed to be about art, peace, and love, and defense is supposed to be all about war—but the music industry is much more brutal than the defense industry."

He says, "Will I ever be in a position where my software engineers are on the verge of a riot because their Critical Design Review is running late? No. But will I be in a position where a disaster is unfolding and I need to not only avert it but somehow turn it into a victory? Yes. I don't avoid or run from these situations. I've learned to steer into them."

It can take guts to engage people in this way when they're angry or upset or scared, because initially they're likely to lash out or melt down. At times like these, it can be hard to resist the urge to escape back to **your here** where it's harder for them to reach you. But as our next influencer shows, this kind of "courage to engage" is a crucial element of positive influence . . . especially when the stakes are life and death.

■ Engaging at a Terrifying Time

Betty Gonzalez-Morkos is a clinical psychologist at Children's Hospital Los Angeles, and she works in a clinic where children get diagnosed with cancer or blood disease.

She says, "It's a scary environment. When the families first hear their child has cancer, the family and the patient go numb and they can't hear anything else. They need to deal with the news that their child is not healthy, and that life is going to change. They need time to truly grieve what they just heard."

She adds, "Even though childhood cancer has a higher remission rate, it's still cancer. We need to give families the time they need to sit with what they've been given, and allow for emotional catharsis, and enable them to deal with the fear. It's not the time to be pushing more information on them right away. The initial meeting for them is a blur. They're on automatic pilot—that's what we hear back from families later."

This is why Dr. Gonzalez-Morkos doesn't jump into treatment issues right then. Instead, she takes time to be emotionally present with her patients and families during the difficult initial meetings. It's not enough, she says, for her merely to hear them out. She has to *get* what they're going through, and they need to get that she gets it.

Dr. Gonzalez-Morkos says, "Being emotionally present is about saying what you feel—giving it a name. If you don't label it—for example, *anxiety* or *fear*—then the families don't think you get it. It's important that they feel emotionally understood. If not, you're just talking. You're not connected."

She notes, "Without the underlying feeling of 'you really know what we're going through' it's just a transaction. You might be sending information, but maybe it's not being received, heard, and absorbed. If you're not emotionally present, they don't feel that sense of connectedness. It seems like you're just going through the motions, just doing your job. It comes across as mechanical, and that you are an authority figure instead of a person with useful information who wants to help and wants the best for them."

She observes, "I've never had a family say, 'How do you know what we're going through? You've never had a child with cancer.'" Even though she's been spared this tragedy, they can sense from the way she engages in **their there**—talking openly about their terror, anxiety, and grief—that she truly understands what they're going through. And as a result, they're willing to entrust the most precious person in their lives to her care.

When you put the three gets of engagement into action, people recognize that you're on their side. They see that you care about their point of view and their preferences, and that you're an ally rather than an adversary. They sense that you're working with them, instead of manipulating or maneuvering around them.

As a result, people's defenses go down, their trust goes up, possibilities open, and solutions appear. That's why the three gets work in nearly any type of situation, from simple one-on-one conversations to challenging encounters where other people are angry, distrustful, or frightened.

Actively using the three gets, however, takes mindful practice. That's because we naturally see things from our own point of view, so engaging in **our here** comes instinctively to us.

To help people see how difficult it can be to break this bad habit, we like to do a little exercise developed by John's mentor and now UCLA colleague, Professor Samuel Culbert. Here's how it works.

> *Imagine that someone in your office gets a promotion. She isn't a personal friend, but you do know her.*
>
> *Now, here's the first question. When you see her, what's the first thing you'll say to her? Everyone pretty much agrees on this. It's "Congratulations."*
>
> *But now, consider this question: What's the second thing you say?*

Professor Culbert makes a bold claim here. He contends there is a single correct answer to this question.

That doesn't seem to make sense to people in his audiences. It's not a math question It's a people question. So how can there be only one right answer?

He asks people to write their answers, and he collects them and reads sample responses aloud. Typically, they sound something like this:

"You deserved it."

"I'm so happy for you."

"You must be thrilled."

"Let me know if there is anything I can do to help you."

These answers seem normal enough. No one would be offended by them. They're safe, and they might even be true.

But not one of these answers, says Culbert, is the right one. He gives his audiences hints: What do all these responses have in common? Who are they really about? Which perspective are they coming from?

The answer is that responses like "you deserved it" and "you must be thrilled" are actually preceded by an implied "I think that . . . ," as in "I think that you deserved it" and "I think that you should be thrilled." So they reflect the perspective of the person doing the congratulating, not the person getting promoted.

Here's where Culbert makes his case for a better answer. He says the best thing to say after "Congratulations" is "What does it mean for you?"

Instead of making assumptions about other people's experiences, Culbert explains, it's more effective to find out what *they* think and feel. Maybe, for instance, the person is terrified about her promotion. Maybe she fears the additional responsibilities or greater visibility to senior management. Maybe she's anxious about the additional work or travel requirements. Maybe she's concerned about her new boss, or other new people with whom she'll be interacting.

The point is that it's her promotion, not your impression about it. So to reach her ***there***, your response needs to be about her—not about you.

Inspired by Professor Culbert, we've done the "What's the second thing you say . . . ?" activity dozens of times with our audiences. The pattern of responses has always been the same.

Except for once.

We were conducting an off-site meeting for a large technology firm, and we led them through this activity. As we read through the responses with the typical answers, we came across one paper that said: "What are the implications for you?" That's essentially the same response as Professor Culbert's "What does it mean for you?"

We announced that for the first time in our experience, someone got the right answer. We read it aloud and asked if the person who wrote it was comfortable talking about it. A woman named Maria raised her hand.

Maria explained that the exact scenario had happened to her in real life. After she was promoted at the company where she previously worked, she received more than one hundred e-mails and voice mails from people congratulating her on her rise to the executive ranks.

She went on to say that all of the messages except one included comments like "It couldn't have happened to a nicer person" and "I'm glad you got this—you're terrific." While those responses were fine, they more or less blended together and she clicked through them quickly.

But there was one e-mail that stood out.

A coworker named Jeff offered congratulations, but then he added, "How do you feel about it?" That caught Maria's attention. Why? Because inside she was deeply concerned about her promotion. She appreciated the recognition and the acknowledgment that the promotion implied. But she also realized her new role called for more hours and more travel, and that didn't fit well with her other priorities outside of work. She was stressed and worried, and she felt trapped by the pressure of her situation. She felt alone and anxious, while everyone else assumed she was exhilarated. Except Jeff.

Maria reached out and asked Jeff to meet with her. Together, they talked through her concerns, which helped her organize her thoughts about how to negotiate the terms of her promotion so she wouldn't be trapped by everyone else's expectations. She now considers Jeff a valued friend and keeps in touch with him, and she told us she's made a habit of asking people, "What does it mean for you?" when everyone else is saying "I'm so happy for you."

The point of this exercise is that we have a natural tendency to come from **our here** even when we're diligently trying to focus on someone else, and even when we think we're succeeding at that goal. Our default approach is to communicate with and influence others from our own perspective, assumptions, and judgments, instead of on their terms. This is a hardwired tendency we can overcome only through active effort.

The best way to accomplish this is to keep the three gets at the front of your mind at all times when you're engaging other people. In every encounter, ask yourself:

- Am I getting who this person is?
- Am I getting this person's situation?
- Am I offering options and alternatives that will help this person move forward?

In addition, keep Professor Culbert's advice in mind. When you're reaching out to congratulate, console, or encourage other people, don't engage them from your perspective. Instead, ask them, "What does it mean for you?" or "What's it like for you?" or "How do you feel about that?" When you do this, you'll open the door to deeper understanding and a more powerful connection—and that leads to real influence.

▶ *Usable Insight*
Don't sidestep a challenging encounter ... steer into it.

▶ *Action Step*
Think about several major turning points in your life: for instance, a promotion, the arrival of a new baby, or a graduation. Next, think about the range of emotions you felt at these times. Were you happy, scared, or anxious ... perhaps all at once?

When you've finished this exercise, think about the other people you know who are currently experiencing important life changes. Then try asking them: "What's it like for you?"

11

Push Their Buttons— Positively

Any reaction is better than none.

Gavin Rossdale, English musician

Engaging people in ***their there*** is a challenge because it takes you outside your comfort zone. And now we're going to suggest something that will take you way, *way* outside your comfort zone. Think of it as "extreme engagement."

This isn't something you need to do all the time. In fact, you'll want to choose your moments very, very carefully. But when all else fails, it can turn an encounter that's going nowhere into a memorable moment that leads directly to a great outcome.

In this approach, you won't just engage another person. You'll *provoke* the person. It's a risky approach, but sometimes it's the only way to get through to a person who's completely disengaged.

To understand why, think about what Marshall Goldsmith—one of the world's best known and most highly regarded executive coaches—defines as the "mojo paradox." Goldsmith notes, "Our default response in life is to not experience happiness. Our default response in life is to not experience meaning. Our default response in life is to experience inertia . . . our most common everyday process—the thing we do more than anything else—is to continue doing what we are already doing."

This is a key reason why real engagement is hard work—and it's also why we sometimes need to make *other* people work at it by shaking them out of their inertia. The goal in this case isn't to force people to move to **our here**, but rather to open their eyes to **their there** and see how they can make their own situation better. Here's how one of our power influencers did it.

■ The Seven Dwarfs Strategy

Karen Salmansohn is a business author and authority on happiness at work. She's sold over a million books, and her catchy tagline is "self-help for people who wouldn't be caught dead reading self-help."

Earlier in Karen's career, before she built the track record she has today, she was interviewing to be a creative director at an advertising agency. Karen's interview time slot came at the end of the day. She could tell that the hiring manager was tired and bored. He'd probably sat through an entire day of asking the same questions and getting more or less the same answers from a long list of job candidates.

He moved mechanically through the interview. At the end, in a monotone voice, he asked the typical concluding interview question, "Do you have any questions for me?"

"Yes . . . " Karen said, and paused, thinking on her feet. To stand out from the competition, she knew she had to do something different.

"What would you like to ask?" he asked.

Karen replied, "Can you name all of the seven dwarfs?"

He did a double take. "What?"

"Can you name all of the seven dwarfs?" she asked again.

"Are you serious?" he asked.

"I am."

He peered at her skeptically for a moment. But he was intrigued and in no hurry to do another boring interview, so he tried to answer.

"Uh, I don't know, let's see . . . there's Grumpy, Sneezy . . . Dopey? Is that one of them? Why are you asking this?"

Karen said, "I'm working on a personality test that involves the seven dwarfs."

"How does it work?" he asked.

Karen gave him a big smile. "The first dwarf you remember says *a lot* about you."

He paused a moment and then laughed out loud. "That's funny!" he admitted. "You got me."

She also got the job.

Now, clearly, this isn't an approach we'd recommend in most job interviews. But it looked like Karen had nothing to lose at that point. And she had a lot to gain by shocking her interviewer into making a connection while simultaneously showing that she had the creativity needed for the job.

Karen's "seven dwarfs" question instantly took her interviewer from bored to curious. She got him to laugh and engage, even at the end of a tiresome day. And she showed that she'd be a great person to work with—someone who could generate ideas and raise people's spirits even under the pressure and strain of long days and difficult projects.

Bold acts like Karen's aren't always successful, but provocation is an excellent idea if you're in a one-on-one situation with another person who's clearly not going to engage with you otherwise. And it's an even better approach if you need to wake up an entire roomful of disconnected people, which is why we frequently play the provo-cateur in meetings and conferences. Here's an example.

■ Engaging the Super-Skeptics

A while back, Mark spoke to a major financial firm's worldwide staff of private wealth managing directors at their Wall Street office. They were arrogant, attention span–challenged, and not people who suf-fered psychological types gladly.

Mark's challenge was to engage this group of very smart people with two and a half strikes on him before he opened his mouth. He figured he had thirty seconds before they disengaged from him.

So he went straight for provocation.

"I'm worth $100,000,000," Mark said immediately, role-playing the part of an investor. (He really doesn't have that much.) "That's down from $125,000,000. When you take a hit like that, you natu-rally begin to think of changing the firm that manages your money. So I'm here because you have an amazing brand." Mark could see the attention in the room perk up.

"However," he cautioned them, "before you tell me why I've come to the right place, let me let you know what you and I already know. Your brochures, websites, mission, and so on look nearly identical to the ones at the firm I'm currently using. Half of you in the room don't even know what your company's vision or mission statement is, and the other half probably don't understand it. And you know as well as I do that the name of the game is 'assets under management' and even though $100,000,000 isn't huge, it's enough to tip the needle in the right direction for your group.

"So here's my question," he finished. "Why should I change to you?"

The audience took the bait and kept taking it. They tossed out answers one by one: "We listen very closely and carefully to our clients' goals and help evaluate them." "We give the very best personalized service." "We can show you proof of how well we've done for clients just like you." "Our research is the best in class." "You've come here because you know how great our brand is and you know how many of the wealthiest people trust us with their money."

One by one, Mark threw their answers back into their faces, showing that they were no different from any other financial firm's responses. They sounded scripted, not passionate.

At the end, he said with full sincerity, "You know, given your company's name, I didn't necessarily expect you to be the 'exotic car' of the financial industry. However, I thought you'd at least be the luxury car. But from your answers—and I hate to say this—you're more like a used clunker ready to be unloaded on the next naïve customer who comes onto the lot. And I think I'm going to keep looking, or maybe even stay where I'm at."

Everyone in the group looked dumbfounded, except the most senior member. He was smiling and even chuckling a little as he watched the audience growing increasingly hostile.

Mark waited until the room was at the boiling point and then said, "Here is what you didn't ask me that would have made a difference."

He began, "First, you were so eager to get my money that you didn't take the time to drill down into my disappointment with my current investment firm. But if I leave them, that's going to be an uncomfortable end to a relationship of a number of years.

"Next," he said, "you know as well as I do that you've lost money for some of your clients, just as my bank did. If you don't know what you did wrong and how you'd do things differently next time, you ought to know."

He added, "I'd also like to know why some of your clients have left you—and if you don't know that, I'd like to speak to them. Look, I don't mind that you've made mistakes; I just want to know that you learned from them and won't keep repeating the same ones.

"Also," he said, "I'd like to know how you treat someone with $1,000,000 instead of $100,000,000—because if you don't treat them as well as me, you're talking about my parents and you should turn them over to people who will. And I also want to know how patient you are at explaining things, because after I'm gone you need to be patient explaining things to my wife and kids."

One of the younger people in the room said, "Our clients never ask those questions."

The senior audience member who'd been laughing piped up, "Yeah, but they could be thinking them!" And on faces everywhere, frowns started changing to rueful smiles.

At this point, Mark's audience was fully engaged. They'd moved from skepticism to anger to "hmmm . . . " and were well on their way to "wow," all because he was willing to provoke them.

Mark knew at the outset that unless he challenged this audience, he'd lose their attention. If he simply explained what he thought they should do (Mark's **here**), he'd lose them. So instead, he gave his audience a firsthand look at a potential client's **there**, showed them how far they fell short of it, and offered them solutions. And in just a few minutes, he took them from bored to infuriated to enthralled.

———

Karen and Mark show that when you're faced with a tough audience and need to prove yourself, provoking them—reversing the tables so that they have to prove themselves to you—can be a game changer.

One of the best ways to do this is to think of someone the audience is trying to win over. For instance, Mark played the part of a wealthy individual his audience would like to gain as a client. At one of the biggest talent agencies in the world, Mark played an actor who was thinking of leaving his current talent agency if the agency he was speaking to could double what he made per movie.

Similarly, if you're training your managers to motivate their people more effectively, you can role-play an unmotivated employee and say, "Why should I get all excited about this new initiative?" Or if you're trying to help your partner understand what's going on with your teenager, you can try role-playing your child's point of view: "So why does some stepparent I'm not even related to have the right to criticize *my* behavior?"

But do be careful, because this approach can backfire if you're not truly connecting with the hearts and minds of the people on whom you try it.

When you engage by provoking, you need to move other people from their first response (fighting back) toward the result you want (buying in). To do that, you'll need to understand *their there* before you even start—and that's where a tip from one of the world's greatest boxers can come in handy.

The story starts with Alex Banayan, a remarkable undergraduate student at the University of Southern California seeking a great outcome: He wants to understand how people became exceptionally successful early on in their careers. Alex is investigating how those early starters got ahead of the curve so he can share what he learns with others. "I want to know what people my age can learn," says Alex, "and what we should start doing now instead of waiting."

Among the many high-profile people Alex has already interviewed is Sugar Ray Leonard, the six-time world champion boxer and Olympic gold medalist. Leonard has also enjoyed a successful business career since leaving boxing behind.

Talking about his boxing career, Leonard told Alex that months before the fight, as is customary, he'd join his opponent at a press conference. What normally happened is that the boxers would show up acting tough, talk trash to each other, then square off for pictures, all done to build publicity and increase ticket sales for the fight.

But when Leonard went to these press conferences, he'd go up to his opponent with his arms wide open and say, "Hey man! I miss you baby!" He would flash a big smile and give the other boxer a hug, a playful squeeze on the arms, or maybe some pats on his back. Everyone just thought this was Leonard being the charming guy he is.

But what he revealed to Alex during the interview was that while everyone thought he was just being personable, what he actually was doing by squeezing his opponent's arms, and by giving him a hug and rubbing his back, was physically assessing his opponent's muscles to see what kind of shape he was in, and what sort of training he was emphasizing. This helped Leonard understand what sort of strategy his opponent was planning—information that would go into Leonard's own plan for the fight.

What does this have to do with you? Simple. When you're engaging, your goal isn't to knock out an opponent but to find common ground with a potential ally. However, when you engage by provoking, you're temporarily assuming an adversarial position. And to do this successfully, you need to be very sure that you accurately identify the other person's real issues and focus on them.

If you come from **your here**, you're likely to guess wrong— for instance, by thinking, "This interviewer doesn't like me because I'm a woman," or "He thinks I'm too young for the job." If you make a wrong assumption, your provocative punch won't connect. Instead, you'll create dissonance, because you think you're being forceful and insightful but instead you sound ignorant and arrogant. As a result, you'll annoy or offend the person ("she doesn't understand me at all") and worsen the disconnect between you.

> So follow the advice of Sugar Ray Leonard. Before you provoke to engage, be sure you're in the *there* of the person you're engaging. Get a good feel for what's really going on, rather than making guesses from *your here*. That way, your punch will be on target . . . and you'll have a much better chance of connecting.

Provoking people to evoke a response is a powerful approach that can quickly turn negative situations around. But use it carefully and sparingly. And remember: The key is not just to provoke other people, but to provoke in specific ways that evoke the three gets of engage.

So prepare *before* you provoke, by focusing clearly on the people you want to engage, what their situation is, and what solutions they need. Go to *their there*, and identify the real reasons for their disconnect. And then confront them not with the intent of hurting, but with the intent of helping them move forward. When you do this, you can engage anyone from bored interviewers to a room of high-powered bankers—and that's real mojo.

▶ *Usable Insight*
Before you provoke to engage, it's a good idea to know how it feels to be on the receiving end.
So . . .
What would you say if we asked you: "Which dwarf are you?"

▶ *Action Steps*
Think of three business or personal encounters in which the person you spoke with was apathetic, antagonistic, or otherwise unreachable. Now, see if you can think of a way you could have "provoked to evoke" in each situation.

12

Engage Across Cultures

Our similarities bring us to a common ground;
our differences allow us to be fascinated by each other.

Tom Robbins, author

Awhile ago, Mark took his first trip to India. He was told the trip would be life-changing—and it was.

Mark was looking forward to savoring exotic dishes, making new friends, and seeing the Taj Mahal. But his journey also opened his eyes to how very different two cultures can be when it comes to influence.

Wherever Mark went—from high-rise offices in Delhi to marketplaces in Agra where beggars and street vendors with monkeys and cobras mingled with the crowds—he discovered that hidden agendas were nowhere to be found. People wanted to help him. They wanted to connect with him personally. When people smiled and said "Namaste," they meant it.

Mark was amazed at the contrast between what he saw in India and the disconnected behavior he frequently encounters in Western countries. There was no envy, no jealousy, and no "zero sum" thinking ("I'm doing extra work for this person, and it's not doing me any good").

Mark isn't alone in recognizing the differences between East and West. Executive coach Keith Ferrazzi says, "The further east we go, the more relationship-oriented business actually is. In fact, in China, in the Middle East, and so on, it's actually crucial that you build a strong relationship before you can begin to transact." In America, he notes, "We're not really interested in deep relationships. We're interested more in transactions."

Transactional relationships don't work when you want to create positive influence, and they're even more likely to backfire when you're trying to connect with people from relationship-based cultures like those of India and China. You can't connect successfully with people who expect warmth and respect if you're trapped in a disconnected, transactional mind-set and stuck in the *here* of your own culture.

Instead, in a multicultural world where you're interacting every day with people from other backgrounds, you need to be able to engage from the *there* of any culture. You can't simply focus on transacting deals from a distance; instead, you need to focus on closing that distance. And as one of our power influencers shows, this is easier than it sounds.

■ The Seven Most Important Words and Phrases for Engaging Across Cultures

Brian Adams is the director of the Griffith University Multi-Faith Center in Brisbane, Australia. With over twenty years of experience working in countries throughout Africa, Europe, North America, and Asia-Pacific, he's an authority on how to engage with others and collaborate across cultures, belief systems, and faiths.

Brian says, "It means so much to most people when you try to address them in a way that's central to their identity." And one of the most remarkable things John learned from Brian is that this is possible even if you know only a few words of another person's language. Brian offered a firsthand demonstration when the two of them stopped for lunch in Colorado Springs at a Middle Eastern restaurant called the Arabica Café.

After they entered, the gentleman behind the counter welcomed them and asked for their order. John started to indicate his choice, but Brian spoke first. He recognized from the man's accent that English wasn't his native language. Smiling, Brian told him the food looked and smelled excellent, and then greeted him warmly in Arabic: "Salaam aleik!"

The man's face lit up. Enthusiastically, he returned the greeting: "Wa-aleikum issalaam."

Brian learned the gentleman's name was Kamel, and that he was born in Lebanon and raised in Egypt. He asked how Brian knew Arabic.

Brian replied, "Ana tikelim bil-'arabiya." He explained that he'd studied it at the university he'd attended and found Arabic to be a beautiful, poetic language. He'd learned more over the years while living in a few countries where Arabic was spoken.

Kamel took their lunch orders, and Brian said thank you: "Shukran."

"Afwan," replied Kamel.

A woman soon came to our table and left an entrée of falafel and hummus for us to share. "Compliments of the manager," she said.

If Brian had simply ordered in English and said "Thank you," he would have blended in with all the other customers. But because he connected with Kamel on his own terms, a routine transaction became a memorable meal.

Brian says that when you take the time to learn another person's language, particularly when you're in the majority culture and their language isn't widely spoken, you pay a great compliment and grant noteworthy respect to the other person. And he explains that it's simple to do this—because if you can master just seven words or phrases in a language, you can create an immediate connection. Here's how.

First, learn how to say this phrase:

"In your language, how do you say . . . ?"

Then learn how to:

- Say the person's name properly in his or her native language.
- Say hello.
- Offer a proper greeting.
- Say thank you.
- Say "I appreciate your time with me."
- Offer a proper farewell when your interaction comes to a close.

Write down what you learn, and keep using the words or phrases. Ask the person you're engaging with to correct your pronunciation. At every opportunity, make the effort to add a few new words to your basics.

It's simple, it's fun, and it quickly breaks down walls. Even if you get it wrong, the person will appreciate the respect and the effort you're making. And it's an even more powerful relationship builder if you follow Brian's four guidelines for engaging across cultures.

First, he says, have courage. Many people are hesitant to reach out to someone from another culture because they don't want to look foolish or cause offense. But the very fact that you're willing to stumble through a few foreign phrases or risk committing a cultural faux pas in order to make a connection will speak volumes about your character.

Second, he says, show respect. You don't need to agree with everything the other person says, but assume that you have as much to learn from the person's culture as that person has to learn from yours.

Third, he says, be curious. Show that you're interested in the other person's history, job, relationships, and life.

Fourth—and perhaps most important of all—exhibit humility and a good sense of humor. Apologize in advance for any inadvertent cultural slips you might make, and then join in the laughter if you screw up. In the process, you'll strengthen bonds with people who may still be trying to learn a new language or adapt to a new culture themselves. And while they may chuckle, they'll admire you for reaching out to them in **their there**.

One of the most famous examples of a cross-cultural verbal slip is John F. Kennedy's inspiring address to the people of West Berlin on June 26, 1963. At that time the Cold War was raging and the Berlin Wall recently had been built, separating Communist-controlled East Berlin from free West Berlin. In what might be the biggest crowd in history ever to assemble for such an event, over a million people gathered to hear the President's message.

If you watch this speech online, you'll see that the most enthusiastic applause and cheering from the crowd erupt when President Kennedy speaks to the people of Berlin in German.

Kennedy was not perfect in his pronunciation. Twice in the speech he says, "Ich bin ein Berliner." His intention was to express, "I too am a Berliner." He wanted to convey the sentiment that he stood with them for freedom against the threat of oppression so near at hand.

But Kennedy famously made a subtle mistake when pronouncing those words, because "Berliner" in German can also refer to a certain kind of pastry. Instead of saying that he was like them in spirit—a freedom-loving native of Berlin—what Kennedy actually said was: "I too am a jelly doughnut."

But the crowd understood exactly what he meant to say. And through their thunderous applause, more than a million people thanked him for his attempt to speak in a way that deeply touched their hearts.

So don't be afraid to have your own "jelly doughnut" moment. Even if you don't get all the words right, you'll be rewarded by the instant bonds you create when you say "Gracias" or "Namaste" or "Spasibo." And like John's friend, Brian, you'll make new friends and achieve great outcomes wherever you go.

> One thing that's greatly appreciated but rarely practiced in multicultural relationships is "preemptive humility."
>
> In essence, when you meet someone from another background, you should say something like this: "If things work out, we are going to enter into a working relationship. One of the last things I would want to do is embarrass you in front of people from your culture and put you into a position of having to explain my rude behavior. So if you will tell me what I must be sure to *always* do and to *never* do so that never occurs, I will be happy to follow your advice. We can even work out a signal you can give me if I'm in danger of acting in some kind of disrespectful manner." Such a gesture will almost always distinguish you from others in a very positive way.

■ Breaking Through the Age Barrier

The cultural challenges we've talked about so far aren't the only ones you'll encounter when you want to exert positive influence. In fact, there's one big challenge that we too often overlook—and it's likely to hit very close to home.

In *The Go-Between*, Leslie Poles Hartley wrote, "The past is a foreign country; they do things differently there." And that's true. While seventy-year-olds, forty-year-olds, and twenty-year-olds may work together, share the same recent events, and live in the same families, they have very different pasts—and in effect, they come from very different cultures. As a result, they often wind up misunderstanding or resenting each other.

As our earlier story about Gina Rudan and her "fat brains" shows, it's possible to bridge the age divide by connecting socially with people who are younger or older than you. But right now, we'd like to talk about breaking down this cultural barrier in a different way: by engaging across generations within your own family or company. When you try this, the results can be remarkable. To illustrate this, here's John's story about what happened when he decided to get to know his own parents better.

> I have a personal mission but I didn't fully understand what it was, what it meant, and where it came from until I got some advice from my dear friend, Jim Adcox. Over twenty years ago, Jim suggested that I do something he'd done with his own parents—ask my mom and dad to write about their lives when they were young.
>
> I asked them, and to my surprise, both responded with enthusiasm.
>
> My dad handwrote over fifty single-spaced pages of tightly cramped script. He began with a joke, "I was born at a very young age . . . " but after that, it was difficult to read—not because of his handwriting, but because of the painful experiences he wrote about.
>
> My dad grew up under challenging family circumstances, and he also contracted a disease as a child which caused him to temporarily stop growing while he was between six and eighteen

months of age. This led to other health problems that would plague him his entire life.

For many reasons, while I was growing up, my father and I had a troubled relationship. But reading about his early years, I learned things about my father I never knew, and we were able to talk to each other with an openness we'd never experienced before.

My dad died suddenly from a massive heart attack less than a year after he wrote those pages. It gave us some precious time to connect that I didn't realize would be so limited.

My mother, who turns eighty-one this year, also wrote expansively about her younger years, using an old, trusty typewriter. Her childhood was even harder than my dad's. And though I was aware of many of the events she wrote about, I'd never seen them through the eyes of a scared little girl.

She was one of thirteen children of impoverished immigrant parents. When she was six years old, she fell down in the street and a utility company truck ran over her leg, cutting the length of the leg open and crushing her foot. An ambulance was called, but it didn't come because of the "bad" neighborhood they lived in. A neighbor took her to a hospital, but they refused to admit her, and she almost died before he got her into a different hospital.

At that hospital, a thoughtful nurse gave my mom a Shirley Temple doll. It was the only toy anyone ever gave her as a little girl. She fell asleep holding the doll in her arms, but the next morning it was gone. Someone had stolen it.

When my mom was eight years old, her mother died, and my mom was placed in an orphanage. Children there shunned her because her foot was permanently discolored and disfigured, and they didn't want to "catch" anything from her.

The pages my mom and dad wrote are filled with heartbreaking events, unfairness, and injustice, but they aren't filled with self-pity, and my parents didn't blame others. Their stories are jarringly straightforward. These things happened. This was their childhood.

As I reflected on what my parents endured in their younger years, I saw that these were two people who had paid their dues—much more than their share—early in life. They deserved a great marriage and great working lives, but they didn't get either of those. Their marriage was troubled, and they both endured hard working-class jobs with a long line of bad bosses.

When I was young, observing the turmoil in our family, I used to tell myself, "I don't want to live like this." But later in life I finally asked, "*Why* are they living like this? Why all the strain, anger, and unhappiness?"

The answer would have been obvious to most people, but I'd been too self-focused to see it. Some of their struggles were rooted in their difficult early lives. But there was another reason they endured it all: So my sister and I could have better lives.

My sister and I are both adopted, and as I grew older I eventually appreciated the significance of their choice to raise us. (They had to work hard to get us—my father was so cantankerous that the first two adoption agencies rejected him, but my mother finally got him to behave well enough to get through the evaluation process. She and I laugh about that now.) Being adopted continues to grow in significance to me as I move through the stages of life and appreciate how lucky I was to have the opportunities I was given by two people who had to fight for all of theirs.

Reading their words, and then speaking to my parents in new ways with more heartfelt curiosity, openness, and empathy, I learned things about them that changed my relationship with them and changed my life. It helped me see significant flaws in my thinking and priorities. It also deepened my passion for the work I do, and my understanding about what's at stake for people in having rich relationships and doing meaningful work. I came to see in ways I didn't before how my mission really starts with them, and in a way, even began before I was born.

In its simplest form, my mission is to help good people win at work and life. By "win," I mean that everyone deserves to do meaningful work, to be proud of what they do, to thrive, and to have satisfying relationships and experiences.

I saw firsthand the cost of trading work life for "real" life—of enduring work as a necessary evil—and the terrible toll it took on my parents' lives. It's my desire to pay forward a debt I can't ever pay back by helping other people discover the opportunities in life that I was given, but my mother and father were denied.

When we break through barriers of geography or language or age—just as Brian Adams did in the Arabic restaurant and John did with his parents—we create new possibilities and identify new paths to great outcomes. In Brian's case, it allows him to bring people of different faiths and cultures together as friends. In John's case, it fuels his determination to help people escape the kind of pain his parents experienced.

As their stories show, connecting across cultures and ages isn't difficult if you're willing to take the first step. At work and in your personal life, make it a point to seek out relationships with people from other countries and backgrounds, and with people who are older or younger than you. Ask these people to be a part of your great outcomes, and offer to be part of theirs.

And within your family, engage your parents or grandparents in an entirely new way. Ask them: "What was it like for you growing up when you did?" "What was different about the world then? What was the same?" "What were the best moments of your childhood? The most frightening moments?" The answers will open your eyes and enrich your relationships.

When you connect in ways like this with people from different backgrounds and ages, they'll offer you new perspectives and new ideas. You'll learn from their successes and sometimes avoid their mistakes. Many times, they'll show you an entirely different way of solving problems or approaching life. And as Mark learned on his trip to India, they may forever change the way in which you view your own world.

▶ *Usable Insight*
What would you want someone from another culture to know about *your* life?

▶ *Action Steps*
1. Identify at least three people you interact with, either closely or casually, who are from other cultures. In a respectful way, ask them for insights into their cultures. In addition, see if they'd be willing to teach you some or all of Brian's seven key phrases.
2. If your grandparents or parents are still alive, ask them to write about their early lives. Read what they write, and see how many details of their stories surprise you.

STEP #4
When You've Done Enough . . . Do More

Real influence doesn't just mean meeting people's expectations. It means *going so far beyond them that you make yourself unforgettable*. It means adding value before, during, and after an interaction, and doing more in all three crucial value channels. And it means going beyond adding value yourself, and seeking creative ways for other people to join in great outcomes. In this section, we'll show you how power influencers do it.

13

Do More Before, During, and After

Great things are done by a series
of small things brought together.
Vincent Van Gogh

When you practice disconnected influence, you go into a relationship knowing exactly what you plan to do. Your goal is to transact a deal—*I get this, you get that*—and then be on your way.

But real influence doesn't work that way. To connect in a way that makes you unforgettable, you need to do more. In fact, you need to do a *lot* more.

To understand why, think back to the last time you helped someone very important in your life achieve a goal. Maybe you helped a friend with a business venture, participated in planning a wedding, or pitched in when a son or daughter moved to a new city.

When you offered your help, it's a good bet you didn't say, "I'll be there to help you from 10 AM to noon—but no longer." Or "I'll pack some boxes, but don't expect me to do anything else." Instead, you spent hours running errands, hanging decorations, or moving furniture. You volunteered for messy, dirty, or difficult chores like cleaning the fridge or transporting the wedding cake. You did it all for free, and you didn't resent a minute of it. And then you looked for more things you could do to help.

Why? Because you automatically do more for the people you care about deeply. In fact, you usually don't even stop to think about it. It comes naturally to you because your relationships with these people matter and you want to strengthen them.

Of course, these relationships are special in your life. They mean more to you than a business connection or a relationship with a casual friend.

But in *any* relationship, you can go beyond what's expected. When you do this, you make a statement about who you are as a person and a professional.

Kouji Nakata, a leadership counselor in Southern California, describes it this way. "It's about not being the main attraction. You look for the angle of help; look for the angle of assistance. It's like being a caring relative, like an uncle who really is taking an interest in his nephew. Look for the way that they can shine and help them do it. Don't be the important piece. Step aside, get alongside them, and help them do great things and help them be happy."

When you do this, you set the stage for positive influence both now and in the future. "Overdelivering" makes you stand out in the moment and makes people remember you later. You become locked in as someone who deserves to be listened to, and people don't wonder whether you have ulterior motives or hidden agendas.

But that's not all—you enchant people as well. Our friend Guy Kawasaki talks in his best seller, *Enchantment,* about this aspect of positive influence. "Enchantment causes a voluntary change of hearts and minds and therefore actions," he says. "It is more than manipulating people to help you get your way. Enchantment transforms situations and relationships. . . . When you enchant people, your goal is not to make money from them, or get them to do what you want, but to fill them with delight."

Doing more is like enchantment on steroids. You've already helped people achieve their great outcomes . . . , and now you're amazing them by going beyond anything they ever expected. Their response will be gratitude, respect, or even awe.

Doing more isn't just a onetime thing but an ongoing practice. For maximum effect, you'll want to focus on three distinct times when you can do more: *before, during,* and *after* an interaction. Here's a look at how power influencers make themselves memorable at each stage.

■ Do More *Before*

When you do more before you even begin a relationship, you're immediately telling people that you're not just in it for yourself. And the influencers we spoke with have discovered an infinite number of creative ways to do this.

For instance, we talked earlier about Tony Hsieh, the CEO of Zappos.com. Under Tony's leadership, Zappos grew into a remarkably successful online clothing and shoe company that was acquired by Amazon.com in 2009 for an estimated $1.2 billion dollars. Zappos is legendary for their phenomenal customer service, which results in tremendous customer satisfaction and loyalty—and they're also legendary for the positive way they treat employees.

Zappos is careful to hire people who are a great fit for the company's culture. The company hires only about one percent of the people who apply for jobs. After the first week of training, new hires famously are offered three thousand dollars in cash to leave the company, no strings attached. They can take the money and walk out the door. The offer stays open for three more weeks.

Even though Zappos makes everyone aware of this offer, almost no one takes it. People love the company. They want to stay because they're happy there. And more than that, they know right from the beginning that Zappos is willing to *do more* for them.

By making this three thousand dollar offer to brand-new employees, Zappos sends an important message. In effect, the company is saying, "We're very glad you want to work with us. It matters a great deal to us that you're happy working here. And if it turns out that we're not the right match for you, we want to part company with positive feelings on both sides. So we're willing to take a financial risk for you."

That's an amazing thing to do at a time when most companies treat employees like interchangeable cogs. And it's one reason why Zappos has one of the most loyal and high-performing workforces in the world.

Clients of Zappos, too, get far more than they normally expect from a shoe store. The company offers legendary customer assistance. And you might be surprised to learn that in earlier days when the company was smaller, Zappos' all-hands meetings were streamed live for anyone who signed up to watch.

We asked Tony if he wasn't concerned about something embarrassing being broadcast live during those meetings, or about giving away information to competitors. He said his staff considered these possibilities. They asked, "Which is more in line with our values, transparent or not?" And again, they decided to take the risk.

When you begin interactions in this way—by doing more, and sometimes even taking a risk in the process—you form instant bonds with people who are tired of being ripped off, manipulated, or given the bare minimum of service. You prove immediately to these people that you have integrity. And they tell other people, who tell still more people. Soon, your good reputation goes viral.

And here's another concept that's key to real influence: You can do more even *before* you have a particular great outcome in mind. In fact, you can do more for complete strangers who have no connection with you at all. Think of this as committing "random acts of doing more."

David Bradford, former CEO of Fusion-IO, fell into a great outcome by doing exactly that. Here's the story behind his breakthrough addition of Apple co-founder Steve Wozniak to Fusion-IO, which helped drive the organization's phenomenal success.

David didn't target Wozniak, or "Woz" as his friends affectionately refer to him. Instead, one of David's random acts of doing more led to a cascade of positive results.

David, who at the time was living in Utah, had a friend whose son was moving into the state and could use some help setting up his law practice. David obliged, helping get the young man connected and raising his visibility in the state.

A few months later, because of this connection, David received a request to speak at the Utah Bar Association. It was in Sun Valley, a five-hour drive for him, and he'd be speaking to a relatively small group of fifty people. Many people would have considered it a complete waste of time. But David cheerfully agreed.

After the speech, he stayed for lunch. As it turned out, the keynote speaker was Steve Wozniak. Out of a group of five hundred people, chance led Wozniak's executive assistant to sit right next to David, and they struck up a conversation. She observed that Wozniak would probably enjoy the opportunity to speak with him, joking that he'd welcome "a kindred spirit from the information technology world in a room full of lawyers."

David and Wozniak spoke, and it turned out that Woz had his

eye on solid-state trends that Fusion-IO was exploring. Later David sent him materials and asked if he'd like to be a part of the advisory board. Wozniak said yes, and then went on to take the role of chief scientist.

Chance? Maybe. But in the bigger picture, the David Bradfords of the world don't think of it as blind chance. They think, "That's how it works." It's about a mind-set that starts not with results, but with relationships. You may not have any clue where those relationships will lead . . . but that's part of the excitement of real influence.

■ Doing More *During*

When you're working with other people to achieve a great outcome, whether it's yours or theirs, it's crucial to succeed at the task you're undertaking. But there's doing the task . . . and then there's turning that task into something greater and even more remarkable. When you do the latter, people remember you. What's more, they want to give back to you—and they want to multiply your positive influence.

Kouji Nakata, one of John's mentors and now in his sixties, tells a story about someone who influenced him in this way. "I did an exercise recently," Kouji says. "I took a look at my life, looking at the turning points. The first person who stood out was a middle school teacher who dramatically changed my life. His name is Lester Tanner."

Kouji was born during World War II in an internment camp in California. He's Japanese-American, and his parents were farm laborers. He thought that his life was going to be about "being a day laborer—picking grapes, something like that." He was failing in school and it didn't even occur to him to have any other aspirations until Lester Tanner, who was a fifth-grade teacher at the time and also the school photographer, invited Kouji to be his assistant.

Kouji says, "Before you went into high school where I grew up, you took an aptitude test, and I scored 86 on that test. According to the standard, a score of 85 or below was an indicator of mental retardation, so they said that I had two options: a track for either auto mechanics or wood shop. And I didn't think any different, except Lester Tanner did, and he said, 'That's not right; you're capable of more than that.'

"He gave me more tests, different kinds of tests, ones that were more spatial rather than verbal. I scored 134 on the spatial test. I also found that I was slightly dyslexic, and I'm just one of those people who doesn't take tests very well."

When Kouji entered high school, Tanner stayed in his life. In addition to spending time with Kouji after school and helping him with his math, Tanner also held him accountable for a higher standard of behavior.

"Like one time when he heard that I'd been caught driving my car around on school grounds, and over the lawn and so forth," says Kouji. "He called me to say, 'I heard about that, and I'm very disappointed.' And those words—simple and brief as they were—really, really struck me, and I never did anything like that again."

Tanner ultimately became principal of the school and helped Kouji get into college as well. Much later, when Kouji finished his Ph.D., he went back to visit Tanner. By that time, Tanner was retired.

Kouji says he said to Tanner, "'All those years ago, and for all that time, you took an interest in me and you saw more in me than I saw in myself, and you encouraged me when I thought I had no options. What made you do that?" Kouji was surprised to see that the question puzzled Tanner.

"It became clear," Kouji says, "that it's just who he was; it's just what he did. He helped young people learn and grow and develop. That's what he did with me, and that's what he does with others as well. I caught my breath when I realized there are lots and lots of others like me that Lester Tanner has helped throughout his career, who are just as grateful as I am."

He adds, "These days people often ask me about my younger years and because I'm Japanese-American and highly educated, and a professional, they assume that I was smart all along and an over-achiever in school, and very good at math and science and so forth. And all of that is just not true. It was due to one man's influence that I took an entirely different path in life."

Kouji says it took him many years to decide what it was that he was really cut out to do. "And it turns out," he says, "it's sort of giving back the gift that I received from Mr. Tanner." He says, "It's the thing that I do really well, as a reflection of what he did for me, and that is to see the leadership potential in others, or to see additional potential in others. To see the things they're capable of doing that they don't see themselves and to be a person who helps them see that; to be someone who says, 'You can do this. I believe in you.' And having someone believe in you, as I know from personal experience, is important. It's *so* important."

In effect, Kouji has inherited Tanner's mission: to help other people succeed in spite of obstacles. He's inspiring a new generation of people, and some of them will go on to mentor others. And it all began with a middle school teacher who decided to do more than what was expected of him.

Another of our power influencers, Renard Wright, offers a similar example of how "doing more" can create a powerful bond that makes people want to reach out to you decades later.

Renard is a business consultant based in New Jersey, where he's also president of the board of directors of the Urban League in Bergen County and deputy commissioner of the Continental Basketball League.

He started coaching basketball for kids informally years

ago when he lived in New York City. He worked with a few underprivileged kids in Queens in a dangerous housing project.

A turning point in his life occurred over twenty-five years ago when he showed up at practice one day and asked, "Where's Damon?" The kids avoided his eyes, and one of them said, "He's not coming coach. He died."

Renard says, "I couldn't believe the words that were coming out of his mouth." He adds, "I don't know if there's anything sadder in this world than a child's funeral."

Renard committed there and then to helping children like these. He wouldn't just coach basketball. He'd *do more*. Using basketball as a vehicle for teamwork and camaraderie, he would steer these children away from gangs and drugs.

"On that day, everything changed. I had to help," Renard says. "I'm fifty-four years old and no one has ever asked me why I'm so passionate about this. It's a dedication to Damon."

Renard's basketball club started with a few kids, and other children would come and ask, "Will you help me, too?" The club grew to over two hundred kids, with Renard running everything on his own time, setting up tournaments, special camps and other events, and getting parents involved in a "concerned neighbors" group.

Many years later, Renard now lives in New Jersey and is heavily involved with education, at-risk youth, housing, and other community building efforts. But lately, with the advent of social media connections, he's been hearing from people he coached as children in Queens all those years ago.

"I got a phone call from one of the original few players, who found me on Facebook," said Renard. His name is Lamont, and he's working in a bank now.

Lamont said, "I just called because I wanted to say thank you."

Renard replied, "Listen, you guys were just as important to me."

"That may be true," said Lamont, "but you need to know something. My father couldn't find time for me, but you did, and it made a difference. I'll remember that for the rest of my life."

Over the years, Renard has heard from many former players who've said, "If not for your basketball club, I'd be dead or in jail."

Renard heard recently from another one of the original players. His name is Jimmy, and he became aware that Renard's own son was going through some tough times. Jimmy called Renard and told him he was living in Seattle with six children of his own.

"Six kids!" exclaimed Renard.

"Yes, but I'm thinking about your son. You tell him he can call me anytime. I'll do anything for him."

Renard replied, "But that was twenty-five or thirty years ago that you knew him."

"Yes, but that's just time, and time doesn't matter," said Jimmy. "We're still a team."

If the two stories we've related in this section sound similar, there's a reason. We've picked them specifically to make a point: The influence created by doing more can last forever. After all these years, Kouji Nakata still considers his middle school teacher one of the most influential people in his life. And when Renard Wright's own son was in trouble, one of the students he'd helped twenty-five years earlier tracked *him* down on the Internet so he could offer his help. To earn that kind of loyalty, you need to work at it—and doing more is the best way to do it.

Lester Tanner and Renard Wright did more in big ways, and their positive influence forever changed the people they helped. But doing more doesn't have to involve life-changing acts. You can also become memorable in small but meaningful ways.

To do this, think about every project you're involved in right now, and ask yourself: What can I do to bring a little more value? What can I do that's a little more than what people usually do in this situation? To help the people around me, is there something else I can do, say, bring, offer, or commit to? Then offer your help fully and generously, without thinking about what you might get in return.

And never underestimate the staying power of even a small act. One friend of ours has referred people to the same neighborhood mechanic for more than a decade because back in his starving student days, the shop's owner occasionally threw in a small repair for free. Another friend tells the story of a sanitation engineer who'd make a point each week of tooting his horn when he pulled up to her house to empty the trash cans, just so her toddler could run to the window and see the "big truck." Although my friend and her husband were broke at the time, they bought the man a special gift each Christmas—and thirty years later, they still remember him fondly.

So think about it. If people as diverse as a basketball coach, a high school teacher, a mechanic, and a sanitation engineer can make a lifelong impression by doing more in an interaction—so can you.

■ Doing More *After*

Once we conclude an interaction, it's natural to mentally mark it as "done" and move on. We're all overloaded with commitments, and it's a relief to cross one thing off our to-do list and forget about it.

But if you want to practice real influence, you need to realize that *doing more* doesn't end when an interaction does. In fact, you can often add tremendous value long afterward. And one of the most powerful ways to do that, as our next influencer shows, is simply by expressing your gratitude.

Warren Bennis is chairman of the Advisory Board of the Center for Public Leadership at Harvard's Kennedy School of Government and a close friend of Mark's. A while ago, he was talking with Mark about his cardiologist, David Cannom, M.D.

According to Warren, Dr. Cannom has saved his life five times by fitting him with a pacemaker and updating it according to Warren's condition. "He's responsible for my living long beyond what my medical condition would have usually allowed," Warren told Mark. Warren and Dr. Cannom have also become friends over the years.

Warren shared a story about a recent dinner he'd had with Dr. Cannom and both of their wives. Warren was thinking of how to express his gratitude. At first, he thought of giving his doctor a case of wine, some tickets to an event, or a similar gift. But then he realized exactly what he should do.

"David," he said, "I was thinking of the best way to show my gratitude to you for saving my life five times, and I finally came upon it. I think the best way for me to show it is to live a long, happy, and healthy life."

When he heard these words, Dr. Cannom teared up. He's a brilliant doctor, and he saves lives for a living, so you'd think he might be blasé about the fact that he's a miracle worker. But Warren's words touched him in a way that a bottle of wine or some opera tickets never could.

Warren's story is a reminder that all of us want to know that we're appreciated. Often, we think our gratitude goes without saying, but, as Warren's doctor showed, that's not the case. Even when people know we're grateful, telling them is a gift of great value.

One of the best ways to express your gratitude after an interaction is what we call a "power thank-you":

1. Thank the person for something specific that he or she did for you.
2. Acknowledge the effort it took the person to help you. For example, say, "I know that you rescheduled your vacation to make this project a success" or "I know it was hard for you to let us include your ex in our wedding."
3. Tell the person how his or her action made a difference in your life.

In addition to expressing your gratitude, look for other ways to extend your positive influence. In almost every case, there's a way for you to add value days, months, or even years after an interaction.

For example, think about people and causes that are important to another person. Can you assist with a person's charity work? Refer clients to the person's business? Lend a hand to someone else who's important in the person's life, as David Bradford did by helping his friend's son establish his law practice? When you do more in ways like this, it keeps your connection alive.

Finally, think forward. One way to do more is to ask the question: Can we do this better in the future? If the answer is yes, share your ideas.

Geoff Cowan is president of the Annenberg Retreat at Sunnylands, a facility designed to accommodate meetings among world leaders. Cowan is also a professor and the Annenberg Family Chair in Communication Leadership at the University of Southern California.

Cowan has adopted a "do more after" practice of looking for improvements even when decisions seem right and things turn out well. He says that after you complete a project or initiative, you should do two things. "First, meet with the team to say thank you and tell them they've done a wonderful job. Second, facilitate a discussion about what you all can do to make it even better next time. If you want to be outstanding, you have to make good people feel good, but you have to not be settled with good."

When you *do more*, always remember that you're not "giving to get." Never see your actions as a prelude to springing an uncomfortable request on another person. Instead, understand that your goals are to build long-term relationships and to make things better.

Also, actively work to overcome the "zero sum" mentality. When you find ways to help other people learn, grow, gain, avoid problems, make progress, and achieve their goals, you achieve something far more important than near-term gain. You form the basis for ongoing results, enriched relationships, and an integrity-based reputation. And that will lead—in ways you can't even begin to predict right now—to real, lifelong influence.

▶ *Usable Insight*
Would you rather conclude a transaction today? . . . Or *do more* to build a relationship for tomorrow?

▶ *Action Steps*
1. Think of the times in your own life when people have *done more* for you. If these people are still alive, give them a power thank-you.
2. Think of ways you can do more *before, during,* and *after* the projects you're currently planning.

14

Do More in All Three Value Channels

You will not be satisfied unless you are contributing
something to or for the benefit of others.
Walter Annenberg, philanthropist and diplomat

One consequence of a transactional mind-set is that you tend to focus much of your attention on money, especially when it comes to business relationships. As a result, when you're evolving from disconnected to connected influence, you may still make the mistake of translating *doing more* into *doing more financially*.

But in reality, the most powerful ways to do more in a business relationship usually don't involve writing a check or donating something expensive to a charity. And in personal relationships, they don't involve giving your children bigger allowances or buying your partner an expensive gift. None of these is necessarily a bad idea. But none of them is likely to create lasting influence.

Instead, the best way to create real influence is to do more in ways that touch people's hearts and minds. Here are three ways to do this:

1. **Expand their thinking (*the insight channel*).** Find ways to help them see new insights, reframe their situation, gather new information, and find new meaning in their lives.
2. **Make them feel better (*the emotional channel*).** Find ways to help them feel encouraged, capable, supported, energized, empowered, successful, happier, or valued.
3. **Take effective action (*the practical channel*).** Find ways to help them take action for themselves or for people they care about. Help them resolve issues, solve problems, build relationships, get projects done, or accomplish tasks.

If these three channels look familiar, it's because they link to the three "gets" of engagement we spoke about earlier. Back then, your goal was to understand where people were coming from. Now, your goal is to make things better for them in ways that will make you memorable. Here are some of our favorite examples of how it's done.

■ Adding Insight

When you offer people a new way to see themselves and the world, you change their lives forever. That's real influence—and as our next influencer shows, it can happen in a single encounter.

The memorable encounter we're talking about occurred at the U.S. Air Force Academy some years ago. At the time, John was an Air Force officer serving in the Center for Character Development at the academy. Paul Bucha came to speak to the new class of cadets, and John had the opportunity to escort him.

Bucha is a recipient of the Medal of Honor, the highest U.S. military decoration. It's bestowed by Congress and presented by the President, and it's awarded for extreme bravery in combat beyond the call of duty.

In his speech, however, Bucha didn't talk about the events that led to his being awarded the Medal of Honor. He didn't tell any war stories at all. Instead, he emphasized that it was essential that the cadets learn, as future officers, to support each other, be there for each other, and care for each other.

Then something happened that is still difficult for John to believe: Bucha asked the entire auditorium of military cadets to hold hands.

After an initial moment of shock, the cadets took the hands of the people on their left and right. And as they sat hand-in-hand, Bucha asked them commit to doing the best they could to learn how to take care of one another.

Because of his reputation as a Medal of Honor recipient, everyone in the auditorium did what he asked. It was an extraordinary thing to see, given that young cadets aren't known for being "touchy-feely" types. John suspects that even if the highest-ranking general at the institution had entered that auditorium and given a direct order for the cadets to hold hands, most of them would have reacted with scorn and ridicule. But no one in Bucha's audience was mocking anything. And no one who was there will ever forget that moment.

By asking the cadets in the auditorium to make this simple but profound gesture, Bucha made them truly *feel* something that they'd only understood intellectually before. He made them understand viscerally that they were connected for life, and they were committed to taking care of each other. It's an insight that almost undoubtedly changed how they viewed their careers and their relationships. And it's an insight that could save some of their lives someday.

Bucha could have given the standard speech the cadets expected to hear. He could have talked about his own battles and his own band of brothers. But instead, he gave the people in his audience a new way of looking at themselves and each other. That's doing more on a stellar scale.

▪ Adding Emotional Value

One of our greatest weaknesses when we practice disconnected influence is that we hide our emotions . . . and we ask others to hide theirs. Sometimes we play on people's emotions intentionally in order to manipulate them, but we don't really know or care what those people are feeling deep inside.

Real influencers, however, want to know where other people are coming from emotionally. And in seeking ways to do more, they look for opportunities to make people feel happier, more fulfilled, and more self-confident.

Heidi Roizen, our next influencer, illustrates our point. She's a talented executive whose focus on helping other people learn and grow earned her the informal title of "mentor capitalist" in Silicon Valley and led the *Harvard Business Review* to feature her as an exemplar of relationship building and mentoring.

After cofounding a highly successful software development company, Heidi served as vice president of worldwide developer relations for Apple Computer and later became managing director of Mobius Venture Capital. Currently, she's a member of the board of directors of TiVo and serves on the faculty at Stanford University.

Heidi believes that you can do more for the people in your life by helping them grow, and that it's important to do this. She says, "If you're not trying to grow, you start stagnating. If you're not going forward, you're not staying the same. You're falling back, degrading. It's easy to get in a rut so deep you're afraid to try." One of her favorite quotes is from Eleanor Roosevelt: "Do something every day that scares you."

As a mentor, Heidi gets great satisfaction from doing more by helping entrepreneurs frame their thoughts, manage their feelings, and take action even in the face of fear and uncertainty. She often finds them paralyzed with indecision. She says, "There's so much uncertainty, it's difficult to know the right thing to do. But as an entrepreneur, making *no* decision is often the worst thing you can do. You get frozen in your tracks."

In these situations, she says, people's fears are nearly always more extreme than the reality. "I walk them through a thought process, step by step," she says, "and that helps them rethink the situation and then take action."

One common technique she uses to help them get unstuck is to ask them this question: What's the worst thing that can happen?

"Maybe you won't make your rent payment," she might tell them. "Okay, will the landlord kick you out immediately? Instead, could the intellectual property you have be worth something? Perhaps you can compensate the landlord that way. Or maybe that won't work, and you'll need to move out of the building, and the landlord will rent to someone else. But maybe it will take him a few months to get someone else, so he'll give you time to try to get it turned around . . . ."

As she helps them deconstruct their fear, it releases its grip. That allows them to think more clearly, get their emotions lined up, and then take action. "Make a decision, then act, then course correct," Heidi says. "That's often much better for these entrepreneurs than freezing up in the situations they face."

This advice, coming from a person of Heidi's stature, is extraordinarily valuable. Thanks to her guidance, dozens of entrepreneurs who might have missed their great outcomes due to crippling fear are succeeding wildly. And it's all because Heidi chooses to *do more* in her mentoring relationships.

> One problem we often see when we come into a company
> is that each person is in a "silo"—sitting alone behind walls,
> not knowing or caring about the problems other people are

experiencing in their own silos. This is bad from a business standpoint, and it's even more toxic to people's emotional health.

So one way in which we add value when we consult with business leaders—especially teams coming to grips with very stressful situations—is to spend time helping them break down their silo walls and see each other as human beings. To do this, we ask them to share the answers to questions like these:

- Where were you born?
- What were your parents like, and how did they communicate with each other?
- What's a seminal event from your childhood that has shaped your personality and your values?
- What's the hardest thing you've ever had to do or overcome?
- Who or what helped you through that time, and how? (This could be a person, religious faith, a book, or anything.)
- What is your greatest shortcoming—one that, if overcome, would lead to your being much more successful?
- What is your greatest strength—one that, if you were able to tap it more fully, would lead to your being much more successful?
- Can you think of a situation during the next month in which you will have the greatest opportunity to overcome the shortcoming you named?
- Can you think of a situation during the next month in which you will have the greatest opportunity to tap the strength you named?
- How committed are you to doing this?

In one meeting like this that Mark led, the answers participants shared with him stunned their colleagues. For instance, one man said that he used to leave at 7:00 every night and everyone would tease him about going to see his mistress. During this exercise, he revealed that he left to fight a losing battle to give his father with Alzheimer's dignity. Half the group started to cry and asked why he hadn't told them. He said, "We don't talk about such things here."

Following that, another man said that during the same period, he used to leave at 3:30 in the afternoon and people would say the same thing about going to see his mistress. His confession was that he was going to get treatment for a blood cancer that is incurable, but was currently in remission. More of the men started to cry and asked him why he hadn't told them, and he said, "Just like Joe said, we don't talk about such things."

After this exercise, the people in this group never viewed each other in the same way again. Instead of seeing each other as chess pieces that either helped or thwarted them, they each felt they belonged to an elite team of special human beings who were strong, who persevered through extreme adversity, and who did the right thing under times of extreme stress. They felt honored to be in such a group.

Similarly, our friend Mark Lefko—whose roles include serving as a troubleshooter for forum groups of the Young President's Organization (YPO) that experience difficulties—adds value by getting people to come together, communicate openly, and share problems, fears, concerns, and vulnerabilities.

He says, "Often the individuals in these groups are used to being the decision maker, the authority figure, the person in charge. But they eventually come to see there is a lot of power in coming together. Many times they don't realize that the issue they have is widely shared, whether it's about an employee that's a risk to their company, or a problem with their children, or a mistake they made that they deeply regret."

He adds, "Whatever the challenges and opportunities might be, it's about being supportive of one another, validating one another, offering insights and perspectives and advice. When one member has an issue, we pull the issue into the group, and everyone learns and gains."

■ Adding Practical Value

Meredith Blake is a nationally recognized attorney and social entrepreneur. Currently, she's the CEO of ProSocial, an innovative agency working with influencers to create social change movements. Among her achievements was designing the social action campaign that accompanied the release of *An Inconvenient Truth,* the Oscar-winning documentary by former Vice President Al Gore.

The film was released the same week that Meredith's first son was born. "Becoming a parent caused me to move from being self-focused to becoming much more selfless," she says. "Long before they could speak, my children were teaching me how to strive to reach my potential."

Meredith's desire to keep growing after becoming a parent put her in a unique position to add significant value when the team at Microsoft cofounder Paul Allen's Vulcan Productions approached her firm with an idea for a PBS series on mental health and emotional wellness. Allen was committed to making a difference with this project, but he didn't know how to create the most positive influence.

Meredith found that point of focus in early childhood attachment. She says, "I was brought up during the era when many were following the tenets of Dr. Spock, who said that children were being manipulative when they cried, and you shouldn't pick them up. It turns out that's wrong. It makes them think they can't count on you.

Instead, children need to create a secure base in a primary relationship in order to gain more stability and independence. The first relationships in life influence everything else. The first eighteen months influence how neural pathways are laid out in the brain, and are extraordinarily important for mental health and well-being."

Working with Vulcan Productions and PBS, Meredith's firm incorporated early childhood attachment into the project and made it a thread that permeates the entire series, titled *This Emotional Life*. Ten million people tuned in to the series, exceeding viewership goals by forty percent. There is also a growing online community with newsletters, webinars, and other free content.

But Meredith had an idea for doing more. "I have two children," she says, "and when I was pregnant and giving birth, I didn't hear anything about the importance of attachment. In the hospital I was given a nylon bag with coupons for infant formula, but no information about how to create more secure positive attachments in children. I'm in a high demographic. How are people with even less resources going to find out what to do?" She was especially concerned about the parents who were the most strapped for cash and had the least time to spend with their new babies.

To address this need, she helped develop a kit for parents called "Early Moments Matter." For families who can afford it, it costs ten dollars per kit, and the revenue is used to generate free kits for people who can't afford them. Meredith's agency helped to create a network with hospital systems across the country. They brought promotional partners on board to help bootstrap the additional money needed to distribute the kits to hospitals and give them to less affluent parents.

By doing more—not just helping Paul Allen and Vulcan Productions find a great outcome with *This Emotional Life*, but expanding that outcome to include thousands of new parents in need—Meredith added exponentially to the value of the project. And in the process, she helped fulfill her most important personal goal: to be a role model for her own children.

"Children absorb so much, their brain is a moving train," she says. "I feel a responsibility not only to feed and clothe and shelter and help them grow, but to lead my fullest life and model that for them."

> When you focus on doing more, your goal is to seek ways to help other people—not yourself. But one of our power influencers offers a practical suggestion for helping others *by* helping yourself.
>
> Larry Senn—chairman of Senn Delaney, an international firm focused on shaping organizational culture—says you can do more for the people in your life by making a stronger commitment to keeping yourself healthy.
>
> This may sound self-serving at first, but it's not. When you're in good shape, you're better able to take care of your family and you're more likely to be around to positively influence their lives in the future. And when you're healthy, you have more energy and mental clarity so you make better decisions both at work and at home.
>
> Larry practices what he preaches. At age seventy, he started doing Sprint-triathlons. He's now seventy-six years old, and runs six triathlons per year.
>
> He says, "It all ties back to purpose. My highest purpose is my family. I have a huge obligation to be able to keep healthy for them, and I need to do an exemplary job of taking care of myself. I need also to do an exemplary job for my clients, and to serve them well I need to be at the top of my game, which requires discipline in terms of fitness and diet and growth and evolution as a person."

By the way, Larry often wins in his age group when he runs triathlons. This year he won in Long Beach, Redondo Beach, Manhattan Beach, and San Diego. "I'm not fast, but there aren't many guys left in my bracket!" he jokes. "In these triathlons they paint your age in giant letters on your calf, and I get lots of comments. It's fun to pass guys in their twenties and thirties on my bike and hear them say, 'Wow! Go for it!'"

Doing more may not make you a triathlon champion or give you the power to make an entire auditorium full of military cadets hold hands. But it will demonstrate, more powerfully than any words or manipulative gimmicks can, that you are worthy of people's attention and respect.

Moreover, as Larry Senn and Meredith Blake prove, *doing more* can be a direct path to helping yourself as well as others. When you go beyond what's expected of you by adding insight, adding emotional value, and adding practical value, you gain new insights into your own strengths and values. You find creative ways to solve problems and discover a greater empathy for other people. You act each day in ways that make you proud of yourself. And ironically, by focusing solely on doing more for others, you transform yourself into a happier, healthier, and more successful human being.

▶ *Usable Insight*

After you interact with people, are they better off than they were before they met you?

▶ *Action Step*

For the next week, hold yourself accountable to a new standard of making *every* interaction—whether it's a business meeting, an exchange with a grocery checker, or a conversation with your partner or child—a value-adding experience. Can you provide insight into a problem? Offer practical help? Or simply make the person feel a little better than he or she did before your interaction?

15

Ask *Other* People to Do More

There is no delight
in owning anything unshared.
Seneca, Roman philosopher

What we're going to say next might surprise you.

We've told you how crucial it is to *do more*. We've told you to do more *before, during,* and *after* an interaction. We've told you to *add value* by offering insight, making people feel better, and providing practical help.

But now we're going to tell you: *Don't do too much.*

Right now, this advice probably sounds a little crazy. But what we're really trying to say is: To exert real influence, don't insist on doing more all on your own. Instead, open your arms to other people who want to help. Just as you've invited them to join in your great outcome, allow them to make it even greater by adding value.

When you do this, these people will contribute ideas you'd never think of on your own. By bringing them into the picture, you increase the chances that a great outcome will succeed, and, in turn, you increase your own positive influence.

And here's another piece of advice: When you look for other people to add value, be careful not to limit yourself to "experts" or people with the same experience and background as you. Instead, look for people from different backgrounds who've done and experienced things you never have. As our next example shows, these are the people who can often *do more* in unexpected and compelling ways.

■ A Guest Speaker Offers Her BEST

Carla Sanger is the President and CEO of LA's BEST (Better Educated Students for Tomorrow). The group focuses on solving the serious problem of "latchkey" kids left to fend for themselves in the afternoon after school lets out.

LA's BEST currently serves twenty-eight thousand children at elementary school sites in Los Angeles, focusing on the schools with the lowest student test scores and the neighborhoods most vulnerable to gangs, drugs, and crime. They have an outstanding track record of reducing crime and dropout rates in the areas they serve.

Carla has forty-plus years of experience as a specialist in children's education policy and advocacy, and many of the group's other members have spent decades in this field. But Carla tells about a time they were influenced deeply by one of their newest, youngest members.

On that day, Carla wanted to see what an orientation for new staff looked like, so she sat in on a session about the organization's values. Carla expected to see an older person running the session—but instead, the leader was a young refugee from Guatemala.

The woman began by taking off her necklace and holding it up for everyone to see. "This necklace," she said, "is really, really important to me. It's my grandmother's necklace, and she had a terrible fate." The woman's grandmother, the session participants learned, had been murdered by the authorities in Guatemala.

The young woman went on. "Think of something that, if you lost it, it would really mean something to you—it would really affect you."

The audience was composed of teens and young adults, and this young woman from another country connected with them instantly. They responded to her question: pictures of their parents, trophies from athletic events, and so on.

"What you just talked about," said the young woman, "is how you value something. Let's talk more about that, because here at LA's BEST, we have values and we hold them very dearly. If somebody broke them, or disregarded them, or stepped on them, we would be very upset, just like you would be upset if someone stole the pictures your parents gave you or the trophies you won. We treasure our values. Let me tell you what they are . . . ."

She went on to discuss each value and describe how to put it into action. She emphasized how to use the values to make good decisions. These values, she told them, were something to be embraced for inspiration, not feared for their consequences.

It was a masterful presentation, as good as Carla had ever seen on the topic. And even though Carla had more expertise and experience than anyone in the room by far, she learned from the young woman right along with the new hires.

After the session, Carla asked the woman how she came up with her presentation. She replied, "I just thought about what I would want to hear to help me listen and be engaged."

Because she was young and vulnerable, and willing to open her heart and talk about her own life, this Guatemalan refugee connected with a roomful of twenty-something Americans in a way that the more experienced staff members might not have. And she did it because Carla's staff was wise enough to get out of the way and let it happen.

Ernie Wilson, the dean of the University of Southern California (USC) Annenberg School for Communication and Journalism, shared another story about one more enormously powerful influencer who cast a wide net when he asked people to do more: former Secretary of Commerce Ron Brown.

Brown was a master at pulling diverse groups together, building relationships, and motivating collaboration. "Every six to eight weeks," says Wilson, "he would take a topic and invite people from the private and public sectors and universities to attend what was essentially a seminar. He also invited people from the White House, the Department of Treasury, the Congressional Budget office, and other government agencies to sit in on these sessions."

In one of these sessions, for example, Wilson remembers former Microsoft CEO Bill Gates talking about the importance of hiring to your weaknesses. "When you do that," says Wilson, "you can turn your weaknesses into strengths by involving a network of other individuals and leading by example how to engage with them."

Brown created new networks of people to get smarter about the issues that were important to his mission in the Department of Commerce. They also helped when he needed to manage issues through the labyrinths of other government organizations.

"He made himself accessible—he talked to everyone at all levels and he listened," says Wilson. "He created tremendous goodwill inside and outside his organization and he continued to generate alternative sources of information—other perspectives on the issues."

Over many years, Brown was a strong personal mentor for Wilson, who recalls him saying, "You have to internalize this— everyone has a story to tell, and it's worth listening to."

▪ The Garden of Good and Even More Good

Like Carla Sanger, Mike Devlin has a great outcome that involves kids. And like Carla, he knows how to invite other people to *do more* so his great outcome can become even more extraordinary.

Mike lives in Camden, New Jersey. Maybe you've heard of Camden, because it often gets national attention—but usually not the good kind of attention. That's because it's one of the most dangerous cities in the United States.

Mike wanted to do something to help change this picture. He wanted to create a place where children could learn, play, and be safe. So in 1985, he started the Camden Children's Garden. In addition, he created a community gardening program. Mike found his great outcome—and it's one that requires the whole community to pitch in.

Camden covers nine square miles and has eighty thousand residents. Mike says, "In Camden we have over twelve thousand abandoned lots, and probably just as many abandoned houses." One by one, Mike and his group are helping residents replace the blight of vacant lots with beauty, nature, and life.

And the community has responded enthusiastically. People pitch in, contribute, and help make things better. They built thirty-one community gardens last year and plan to do as many or more this year. Mike observes, "Beautiful areas are less attractive to gangs and drug dealers. A flower can push out a drug dealer."

He adds, "Gardening is a positive activity. Not a lot of fighting goes on in the gardens. Kids who would otherwise be in gangs join our program and get job training and stay in school."

Because sixty percent of Camden's kids drop out of high school, they're not very employable. So Mike's group also created a youth job training program—but a condition of participating is that children can't drop out of school. So Mike's asking them to do more than just garden. He's asking them to succeed.

Mike's group members are continually adding value to their projects, and so are Camden's residents. Mike says, "I've seen community groups go from gardening to restoring homes in blighted areas. They buy them up and fix them up and plant trees. It's a natural renewal that takes place. It might have started by planting a seed. A lot of the language we use about making things better comes from horticulture. It's the language of gardening to plant a seed, to grow, and to make something beautiful."

We spoke with Marchelle Roberts, who is one of three generations—along with her mother and grandmother—working with the Children's Garden. "When the garden first opened," says Marchelle, "my mother had us volunteer at festivals and get involved." Marchelle went on to work at the garden through its Youth Employment and Jobs Training program. Later she went to Temple University, where she's currently a senior.

In the summers, Marchelle comes back and works at the Children's Garden. She says, "I've grown up here; everyone is like family. They've known me all my life, and they have been looking out for me, for my better good." She adds, "It makes a difference to know I'm part of one of the good things in Camden. People often don't focus on the good things."

Mike and his group are a living example of a philosophy we heard from another influencer: Jonathan Fielding, the director of the Los Angeles County Department of Public Health.

Fielding says, "There's nothing more divisible than credit for accomplishment. It's much easier to build coalitions and be part of something bigger and better than oneself. Credit is infinitely divisible." When people heap praise upon him for the results

he's achieved, he says, "What we did was the result of great
partnerships. We were part of a large group. Let me tell you who
they are and what they did. . . ."

At opposite ends of the country—one in Los Angeles and the
other in Camden—Carla Sanger and Mike Devlin are helping to
change the world for at-risk children. They're succeeding because
of their expertise and their passion, but they're also succeeding because they're inviting other people to add value.

When you do the same thing yourself, you'll take doing more
to a whole new level. In addition to going beyond people's expectations, you'll bring in other creative, inspired people who can magnify the success of an outcome beyond your own expectations. And
the more diverse your group of "do more" people is, the more remarkable the results will be.

So search outside your own group of colleagues, friends, and relatives. Reach out to people or groups you've never contacted before, and
pull in participants from all walks of life—not just experienced pros,
but also newcomers who can offer exciting "out of the box" ideas. Ask
them to make a great outcome even better by offering insight, helping
people grow emotionally, and pitching in to provide practical support.

And then, when people point to your success, say, "Let me tell
you who made it happen and what they did. . . ."

▶ *Usable Insight*
To add value, let *others* add value.

▶ *Action Step*
Make a list of the great outcomes you're involved in now and the
ones you're planning. For each outcome, identify at least five people
who may be able to *do more* to make the project a success. Focus
in particular on people who may be able to bring a very different
perspective to your problems and goals.

Taking Real Influence
to the Next Level

When you practice connected influence in challenging times, you can transform vulnerability into triumph, create a lasting legacy, and repair even the most damaged relationships. In this section, we'll show you how. In addition, we'll tell you why gratitude is one of the biggest keys to becoming a "power influencer."

16

Let Adversity Lead You to Great Outcomes

Kites rise highest against the wind—not with it.
Winston Churchill

Millions of people fail to achieve great influence because they're stuck in "I can't." They have a host of highly persuasive reasons why they can't create great outcomes and get others to buy into them:

I'm too weak.
I'm too poor.
I'm too powerless.
I'm trapped too deeply in grief.
I'm too scared.

But the truth is that our own setbacks or tragedies often lead us to missions that change our lives or even the world. Look around you, and you'll see hundreds of examples. An injured soldier and his friends and family started the Wounded Warrior Project. The Susan G. Komen Foundation raises millions of dollars in honor of a young woman who died of breast cancer. A first lady who triumphed over substance abuse founded The Betty Ford Clinic. A man who lost his sight in a devastating accident invented the Braille language. A family whose child was near death discovered Lorenzo's oil.

In our careers, we have been privileged to know dozens of positive influencers who were able to turn adversity into great outcomes like these. Many of them started with little or no money. Some were ill. Some were recovering from abuse. Others were battling demons like mental illness or substance abuse.

One common thread in all of these people's stories was their determination to bring something positive from their experiences. A second common thread is that they were able to get out of *their here* and move to the *there* of other people in need. And a third is that many of them took a powerful first step: They shared their vulnerability openly.

Here, for instance, is the story of how one physician overcame crippling fear and insecurity—and, in doing so, created a movement that changed the lives of doctors around the world.

▪ Bringing a Secret Out in the Open

Danny Friedland, MD, is a founding father of Evidence Based Medicine (EBM), a worldwide standard for medical care. He published the first U.S. textbook on EBM in 1998, and he went on to train thousands of physicians in this life-saving methodology. That's a great outcome, but it's not the one we want to talk about here.

Many years before he became famous in his field, Danny did his medical school training at the University of California at San Francisco. He had a difficult time. He was an immigrant from South Africa, and he felt terribly isolated. He sought counseling, but he says the only thing he remembered after six months of sessions was being told, "Sounds to me like you got your lid flipped."

Danny didn't know what to do. But he knew he was scared too much of the time. And he decided to face his fear instead of hiding it.

So he started talking to other medical school students. "Do you have self-doubt?" he asked. Most of them said, "Yes, of course." He interviewed 314 people, and 311 said they struggled with significant doubts about their self-worth.

What he came to find was that sixty percent of the seemingly calm, confident overachievers he talked with went into counseling by their second year, just as he had. He wasn't isolated in feeling alone and scared. Most of his peers felt that way. And all of them were living on the brink of a breakdown.

Paradoxically, Danny found power, creativity, and inspiration in this knowledge. Rather than retreat, he went for a great outcome.

Danny reached out to his fellow students, letting them know they weren't alone in their fear and doubt. He created a special student network where aspiring doctors could share their stories and talk about their vulnerabilities. In the process, he changed the culture of the entire school. He went on to give leadership training in vulnerability to other students, and then he was asked to train doctors. Eventually, he influenced the entire medical community. And in light of the high rate of suicide and depression among stressed-out doctors and medical school students, he's no doubt saved the lives of many of his colleagues.

Danny's victory illustrates the most important rule for influencing when you're vulnerable: *Acknowledge your feelings*. Because when you do, you can address them effectively.

When Danny faced his own fear and self-doubt, it gave him the strength he needed to look beyond his own **here** and engage other doctors. And when he did that, he discovered that they all had a blind spot. Each one thought he or she was suffering alone in a sea of bright, confident, self-assured peers. By asking a simple question—"Do you have self-doubt?"—Danny was able to see past that blind spot and create a great outcome.

What's the moral? When you're in a vulnerable position, realize that you're not alone. No matter what you're experiencing, there are others who've been where you are . . . and, together, you may be able to achieve a great outcome. And often, the first step is simply to ask: "Is anyone else out there scared?"

Many years after his medical school days, Danny once again needed to transform a terrible time into a meaningful outcome when his mother became very ill. She was seventy years old at the time, and had always been vital, healthy, and energetic. Now suddenly she was losing weight and fatigued. Those symptoms, along with her loss of appetite, led Danny to suspect cancer. Her physician, however, didn't seem interested in working her up, and was about to go on vacation.

Danny pressed for tests. The gastroenterologist said the results were negative and it was just psychological. Danny had to fight for a diagnosis. He got the doctor to run a CAT scan, and when the radiologist called him with the results, it was terrible news. His mother had pancreatic cancer, and it had spread to her liver. Danny broke down, because he knew his mother would be dead in a few months.

Danny says calling his mother was the most difficult thing he ever did.

He phoned and said, "I'm so sorry about what I have to tell you." She replied, "It's the silent killer, isn't it?"

He flew to San Diego to be with her. When he arrived, he held her and said, "No matter what happens, I promise you this will be the richest year of your life."

Danny took her to see her oncologist. He says, "I've never seen anyone with worse bedside manner. I handed over the research about treating this stage of cancer. It was clear he was not up on the latest information. He was saying 'this is interesting' instead of 'this is what we should do.'"

Then the oncologist turned to Danny's mother and said, abruptly: "Tell me, do you want chemo or not? What will it be?" She was trembling. Danny took her from the office and said, "You'll never see that man again."

He did some research and took her to Dr. Laurie Frakes. The first thing Dr. Frakes did was open her arms and say, "Around here we're hugging kind of people," and she embraced Danny's mother, who told him later, buoyantly, "That woman is a pill!"

Danny and Dr. Frakes collaborated on his mother's care. The median survival rate was four to six months, but his mother lived fourteen months and improved her quality of life dramatically. She went from extreme fatigue to being able to work out four days a week. She never spent a night in the hospital and never had intense pain.

That was an unexpected and welcome result, but it wasn't the only one.

The extra time gave her and Danny's father room to grow. His father used to withhold his affection and withdraw. But now he found a new tenderness in himself and started reaching out, holding Danny's mother's hand. He doted on her in a way he'd never done.

And Danny's mother changed, too. She used to crave attention and be easily upset when she didn't get it, but now she radiated affection and wanted to be connected with her family.

The relationship between Danny's mother and father blossomed. After eight weeks, she asked, "Where will I go when

I die? Where am I going to?" His father said, "Wherever you go, our souls will be intertwined."

Danny's journey with his mother changed his life. Helping her find the best medical information; navigate the healthcare system; manage her stress and uncertainty; find new meaning, motivation, and purpose in her life; and then die well—all of these led Danny to the work he currently does, which focuses on helping other patients have a positive experience just as his mother did.

■ Letting a Great Outcome Find You

As Danny's stories demonstrate, pursuing a great outcome can require enormous courage. And that courage can take many forms—one of which is stepping into the unknown.

It's hard to leave one path in life and choose another because it's tempting, both financially and emotionally, to stay with what's "good enough." But when an initial direction disconnects you from your ideals and passions, it's time to think about whether "good enough" is enough.

One person who did that is David Levinson, the founder of the California volunteer organization, BigSunday.org. When we talked with him, David told the story about how he came to start Big Sunday. It's a story about a great outcome finding *him*.

David was a screenwriter in Hollywood. Anyone who's worked in Hollywood knows how challenging the entertainment industry is, with a well-earned reputation for people with sharp elbows and selfish motives.

After years of working hard to achieve a well-earned level of success in this career, David had a revelation. It came to him after a major producer called him in for a meeting.

The producer liked David's writing and wanted to hear his ideas for a scripting a movie idea. But in the meeting, the man focused instead on attacking a greasy batch of roast chicken without utensils while looking only at his computer instead of David.

There was David, watching this person slobber over his meal, while the work he'd put so much effort into creating seemed to be an afterthought on the agenda. David heard that the producer loved his pitch, but then he heard nothing more—total silence.

David says this sort of treatment isn't unusual in Hollywood, but "sometimes something hits you at the wrong time in the wrong way." He didn't like the side of human nature that this episode revealed, and he didn't like having his fate in the hands of people like this self-absorbed executive.

While continuing his screenwriting, David decided to redirect his frustration toward volunteering to help others in need. He began taking on more and more responsibility for helping with events at his synagogue . . . and things started falling into place.

Watching his staff of volunteers grow, and driven by the core belief that *everyone* has some way that they can help someone else, he came up with a magnificent idea. As he explains in his book, *Everyone Helps, Everyone Wins,* he decided to pick one day a year to focus on—a day that would be open to everyone, with no religious or political affiliation or agenda. That was "Big Sunday."

What started out as one day of volunteering for a worthy cause in southern California has expanded into a series of community events throughout the year. It's grown from a single-day event into a three-day weekend that attracts over fifty thousand people from throughout California. Last year on Big Sunday Weekend, tens of thousands of volunteers gave away more than eighty-five truckloads of clothes, books, food, furniture, musical instruments, luggage, toys, and other items.

Think of that . . . fifty thousand people each year volunteering their time and effort over several days for a common cause. And all because one person channeled frustration into passion and decided that "good enough" wasn't good enough.

Robin Kramer is another power influencer who walked away from a bad outcome and found a great one. As a result, she became the first female chief of staff for the mayor of Los Angeles and served as chief of staff for both Republican and Democratic administrations, engendering respect that spanned party lines and parochial interests. (As she put it in a guest lecture in John's class, "Potholes are not partisan.")

Years ago, Robin worked as the head of volunteers on a statewide California campaign. She grew tired of watching people compete for power, vying for the favor of the candidate and positioning themselves for top jobs while shoving other people aside. She had visions of public service, but it wasn't working out for her.

So she decided to quit. She knew there must be a better way to pursue her aspirations for public service.

She told her boss that she'd found a replacement who wanted the role, and she was leaving.

Her boss said, "You can't leave. The election is coming soon."

She said, "My replacement is ready, willing, and capable, and will do a great job."

Her boss—obviously a believer in disconnected influence—repeated, "No, we need you. You can't leave."

She responded, "Yes, I can leave, and I *am* leaving."

"You *can't*."

"Yes . . . I *can*."

As negative as her boss's approach was up to this point, his next move was worse. He said, "If you leave, you'll never work in politics again."

Robin left. And as her influential career testifies, she wasn't done with public service. She was just getting started.

Robin says this was the worst job she ever had. "But in another way," she added, "it was also the best job I ever had, because I found my voice. I said no to a powerful person, I meant it, and I made it stick."

David and Robin found their great outcomes by letting go of bad ones. And if the life you're leading now leaves you stressed and miserable and your passion vanished long ago, maybe you should think about making the same move.

When we talk about having the courage to step into the unknown, we like to share a story our friend Stefan Swanepoel tells.

A world traveler born in Kenya and schooled in Hong Kong, Stefan immigrated to the United States two decades ago without knowing a single person in the country. Today, twenty books and influential reports later, he's widely recognized as the leading authority on trends in the residential real estate brokerage business.

In his best seller, *Surviving Your Serengeti: 7 Skills to Master Business & Life*, Stefan returns to his roots in the Serengeti. The first lesson he focuses on surprises many people.

"In the Serengeti plains of East Africa," he says, "a land suspended in time, the last refuge of the greatest concentration of animals on this planet, there is one species that dominates, and few people who don't live there know which one it is."

He continues, "It's not the largest animals, such as the elephants or rhinos. It's not predators such as lions, cheetahs, or crocodiles. It's the wildebeest, an animal that many people haven't even heard about. The wildebeests dominate the Serengeti. Millions of them journey over one thousand miles every year, and life on the Serengeti revolves around their migration. Their endurance, tenacity, and resilience enable them to dominate the entire landscape."

That's what triumphing over adversity is all about: endurance, tenacity, and resilience. If you have all three—along with a big dose of courage—you have the tools you need to survive. And that's not all. You also have the power to wield positive influence, to turn setbacks into successes, and to say "enough" to dead ends and find your own Big Sunday.

▶ *Usable Insight*

> *If you think you can or think you can't, you're right.*
> Henry Ford

▶ *Action Step*

Think about a hardship or setback you or your family members are facing. Then ask yourself: Is there a way to find a great outcome in this situation?

17

Influence by Getting Out of the Way

*"Being humble is not thinking less of yourself,
it's about thinking of yourself less."*
Tony Hsieh, CEO of zappos.com

When you achieve a great outcome—especially a big one—it becomes part of you. You've invested time, sweat, and perhaps even tears in creating something that's amazing. Your accomplishment changes the way you define yourself and the way other people define you.

At some point, however, the time may come to let someone else continue your legacy. This can be wrenching, because—like leaving home when you reach adulthood, or watching your own child go off to college—it means letting go of a part of yourself.

But if you're strong enough to get out of the way so others can take over, you can ensure that your great outcome lasts forever instead of vanishing. And that's why letting go is a challenge that power influencers are willing to face head-on—as our next story shows.

■ Saving a Great Outcome by "Strategically Getting Out of the Way"

John worked for several years with John Rawling, the former CEO of Robertson Fuel Systems, and considers him one of the finest leaders he's ever known.

CEOs talk of the need to be "always on" because people are constantly observing them and taking cues from their behavior. John Rawling was one of those rare individuals who never had to try to be "on" because he was always unfailingly genuine. Things were never transactional with him—everything had a personal touch. Every conversation with John was connected. If he was talking to you about something, it mattered to him. You mattered to him.

John had a booming voice, an imposing presence (he was 6'5"), and a larger-than-life personality, but he exerted strong positive influence without wielding an imposing ego. He didn't talk about what he wanted people to do for him. Instead, he focused on the company's mission, their customers, and the people in his organization.

Several years ago, even though the company was performing strongly and earning fanatical customer loyalty, John realized that it should change its strategy in the future. To keep growing, the company needed to broaden its customer base and product offerings. John knew that eventually the company would need a new leader as well—and he decided it was time for that new leader to start taking charge.

John could have stayed much longer in the CEO position he loved, leaving it to the board of directors to plan for his succession later. But he didn't think that way. Instead, he thought about what would work best for everyone else.

John found an ideal candidate in current CEO Tom Harrison. John personally lobbied hard to find a way to bring Tom on board, and he succeeded. John planned on staying about a year to ensure a smooth transition—but after a few months, when he saw that Tom had things well in hand, he "strategically got out of the way." While he loved the company and its people, he knew the transition would be smoother if he left.

In retrospect, John's selfless act turned out to be prescient because the time he actually had left turned out to be short. In a terrible shock to everyone who knew him, he passed away suddenly and unexpectedly due to complications from minor surgery. His family, friends, and employees grieved deeply at the tragic loss. But his company was able to weather the tragedy because the new CEO had things firmly in hand.

> Like John Rawling, the power influencers we interviewed are always aware of the need to help others step into their shoes.
>
> Another person we spoke with is Hank Kennedy, the president of AMACOM, the publisher of this book. In one of our talks, Hank said that he's always believed that it was his responsibility to find and train his replacement before he moved on to the next job. And he's doing it again now, for the last time. He said, "I just turned sixty-six, and I probably have between two and five years left working. My job now is to find and train my successor."
>
> That's true humility. And it's an attitude that sets real influencers apart from the people who focus on short-term wins rather than lasting legacies.

■ Helping Others Find Their Great Outcomes

Sometimes getting out of the way means handing off a great outcome. Other times, it means saying goodbye to people who helped you make your outcome happen. When new opportunities open up for these people, it's crucial to help them find success—even if it will be hard for you to replace them. In fact, as our next influencer shows, you can actively help them make the decision that's right for them.

Years ago, a good friend of ours named Glenn Rupert worked at Florida Rock Industries, a family-run concrete and aggregate business. Two things that attracted Glenn to the company were its leaders' reputation for integrity and the high standards of conduct employees were expected to uphold.

Those standards started at the top. For example, one Monday morning owner Ted Baker accepted a handshake deal for a certain price on a crane he'd put up for sale. Later that day, another man offered him almost double the price. Baker said he already had a deal, turning down hundreds of thousands of dollars—all on the basis of a handshake.

Glenn says, "These were the kind of people I worked for, and *wanted* to work for—people who could be counted on to do the right, common-sense thing, all of the time."

Glenn talks about a time he went in to see his boss, Diggs Bishop.

"I'd met a human resources consultant the day before," says Glenn, "and I began talking about what she did for a living and how much I admired it. She was an independent consultant, and I was talking about that, too—the variety of organizations to see and learn about. I guess I was going on and on about it, because at one point Diggs held up his hand and said, 'Glenn, I have a question for you.'"

"What is it?" asked Glenn.

"What do you want to do?" asked Diggs.

Glenn thought he was changing topics and started talking about a current project, but Diggs said, "No, I'm not talking about that. I'm talking about you. It sounds like the sort of work she's doing is very appealing to you. What do *you* want to do?"

Glenn said he'd love to do what she did, helping people grow and develop and change. But he couldn't see himself being successful in that sort of role. He saw himself much more as a project execution guy.

Glenn says he remembers to this day Diggs shaking his head and smiling at him and telling him he was wrong. He said, "Glenn, you're as good as anyone could be in what you do now, and I'd hate to lose you. But you can be wildly successful doing whatever you want. You just need to choose what it is, and decide to do it. You give it some thought, and tell me what it is, and I'll support you and help you, whatever it is."

Glenn says that conversation was a big part of his decision to quit a very successful job with wonderful leaders and go out on his own.

That was ten years and many happy clients ago, and Glenn is going strong in his new career. And it turns out he had an additional reason for wanting to change direction. Glenn married the HR consultant he'd told Diggs about . . . and that's still going strong, too.

———

Throughout this book, we've said that real influence is a way of *being* as a person and a professional—not a way of calculating short- and long-term advantage. Because of their belief in this principle, John Rawling created a powerful legacy and Diggs Bishop created a strong reputation for integrity. And neither one was afraid to influence by getting out of the way.

Doing this isn't easy, because it means setting your own ego aside. But by stepping aside gracefully at the right time, you actually *expand* your influence. That's because people admire your integrity and selflessness and are even more willing to buy into your future goals.

And speaking of those goals, here's something else to think about if you reach a point when it's time to hand off a great outcome. John Glenn, the first American astronaut to orbit the earth, later became a U.S. senator. John Grisham had a successful career as a lawyer before he became a best-selling fiction writer. And Grandma Moses, one of the world's most famous artists, worked on a farm until old age forced her to retire and take up painting full-time.

So when it's time to say farewell to one great outcome, consider this: Maybe you're just opening the door to the next one.

We talked earlier about Mike Critelli, the inspirational CEO of Pitney Bowes. When Mike retired, he didn't stop inspiring. Instead, he took on a very different sort of project, energized by his passion for encouraging future leaders in all walks of life.

Recently Mike produced a film called *From the Rough*, based on the true story of Tennessee State University's Catana Starks. Starks was the swim coach for TSU in 1988 when, in accordance with Title IX, the Board of Trustees eliminated certain teams and created others.

Swimming was eliminated, and Starks found herself out of a job. So she applied to be the coach for the newly formed men's golf team, and she got the job. As an African-American woman, and the first female head coach of a college men's golf team, she faced daunting challenges but overcame them with spectacular results. She recruited a team of underprivileged young people from around the world and led them to set a record at the PGA National Collegiate Minority Championship.

Mike didn't need to pursue this project—but he did, because he wants Catana Starks's story to inspire thousands of people to challenge the status quo and do "impossible" things. And well after his retirement, Mike himself is continuing to inspire people by multiplying his positive influence.

▶ *Usable Insight*

How many great outcomes do you think you have in you?

▶ *Action Steps*

1. If you are a department manager or CEO, sit down with the key people around you and challenge them to envision extraordinary success for your team or your company three to five years down the road. Brainstorm with them about what you can do to achieve that success. Encourage them (and yourself) to think less about you in particular and more about any person who might be in the position you hold—what would *that* person most need to do?

2. Think about the future paths of the people in your personal and professional life. What do they want to do, what are they capable of learning and doing, and what possibilities might be within their reach? Find a way to explore these questions with them.

18

Influence Positively After You've Made Big Mistakes

*Real leaders talk openly about their failures.
They never hide them, because they know
that's where the best learning comes from.*

Robert Fiske, trusted adviser to CEOs

In an ideal world, we'd all be ideal people. We'd never act stupidly, say hurtful things, lash out blindly, or behave unethically.

Of course, that world doesn't exist. All of us screw up occasionally—and sometimes we do it on a grand scale. To repair the damage, we need to learn how to make things right after we've made them wrong.

This is even more crucial if you've spent years practicing disconnected influence. Tricks and manipulation can leave a trail of hurt and anger that will mar your reputation and relationships forever unless you take steps to change things.

This isn't easy, and the first step is the toughest one: facing your mistakes head-on. Here's the story of one person who was brave enough to do that.

▬ Bunt Signs

John once coached an executive named Steve who used sarcasm and a sharp sense of humor to point out the flaws in other people's ideas and push his own agenda. His mocking jibes often made people laugh, and so he didn't see a problem. But his team did.

Confidential interviews revealed that Steve's peers and the people who reported directly to him resented his behavior but didn't want to appear "weak" by complaining about it. The people he targeted for his biting remarks often felt embarrassed and upset. Others were uncomfortable, too, and wary of becoming the next targets. Steve was damaging his relationships and demotivating people who worked with him, and it was taking a bigger and bigger toll on his firm.

When John gave Steve his colleagues' feedback, he took it well. He hadn't realized how hurtful his actions were, and he truly wanted to change his behavior. But he struggled because he wasn't always aware when he was making mean-spirited remarks until it was too late and the damage was done.

Steve asked some of his key people for help, telling them that he wanted to change. This was a good first step—but he needed to demonstrate his commitment, and find a way to do it consistently.

So Steve and the people he spoke with worked out a system. If they saw him starting to make sarcastic remarks or otherwise embarrass people, they'd signal him secretly.

And it worked. Steve would start telling an embarrassing story, and one of his helpers on the other side of the room would rub a shoulder or scratch a rib. Steve would see the signal and bail out of the cutting remark he was about to deliver.

"It became an inside joke," Steve said. "Instead of me making fun of others, the joke was on me. I had people in meetings helping me avoid being a jerk. They were like third-base coaches in baseball, signaling the batter to bunt the ball. Come to think of it, that's a good analogy. They helped me to stop striking out so much by taking wild swings, and instead, to advance others into scoring position."

Steve's openness about his problem, his willingness to take responsibility for the consequences of his behavior, and his positive spirit about enlisting help from others paid off. Even the fact that he asked for help, and the *way* he asked, earned him some goodwill. When he followed through, he earned more.

"At first, I was getting lots of bunt signs," Steve laughed. "I saw a lot of itchy ribs out there. But fortunately they realized I really meant to change, and they were willing to help, and I started to get it through my thick skull that you have to think a couple steps ahead about how your actions stick, especially if they cause unnecessary agitation in others."

Steve was able to repair his business relationships—even after years of behaving badly—because he had the courage to stop seeing things from **his here** (I'm forceful and witty) and instead see them from his team's **there** (Steve is a jerk). He did this again when he asked his "coaches" to tell him when *they* thought he was striking out.

And there's another big reason Steve turned things around: He had the courage to face up to his own mistakes.

Often, we shy away from doing this, because we're too defensive or too ashamed to look honestly at the stupid things we've done. But mistakes don't make us weak or bad—they simply make us human. And as our next power influencer shows, even the best of us sometimes need to make amends.

■ A Hero with an Achilles Heel

Gus Lee recently completed a tour of service as Chair of Character Development at the United States Military Academy at West Point. Earlier in his career, Gus was a drill sergeant, served as a paratrooper, was commissioned in the infantry, and later became an Army lawyer. He received two Meritorious Service medals and an Army Commendation medal. He served two tours of duty as a soldier in the DMZ in Korea and jumped with the Republic of Korea Airborne. He also served as legal counsel to the U.S. Senate Armed Services Committee's worldwide Connelly ethics investigation, and has written several best-selling books.

He held a number of other public and private sector senior leadership positions, and also sadly (to him) became a three-time corporate ethics whistle-blower. Gus has resigned from boards to protest ethical misconduct and has been fired for taking ethical stands.

That's a remarkable list of great outcomes. But Gus rarely talks about his accomplishments. Instead, he writes and talks about his mistakes.

As a cadet at West Point, Gus was mentored by Norman Schwarzkopf (who would go on to become a world-famous general after a stunningly rapid victory in the Gulf War). At one point, Schwarzkopf called him out for getting by on humor and charm and being clever. "You're going to end up with fifty-five armed men who are going to rely on your every move and your character," he said to Gus. "Are you ready for that?" Gus knew he wasn't, and asked for help.

Schwarzkopf told Gus how he'd learned his own life lessons, and what he revealed was surprising. This big, powerful Army officer told Gus that being forthright about one's faults and admitting vulnerabilities are keys to growing as a person and a leader. He told

Gus of his own struggles and insecurities. He showed him how to recognize that understanding his weaknesses was the beginning of strength.

Another role model for Gus is his wife Diane, who also coauthored their book *Courage: The Backbone of Leadership*. Among other things, Diane transformed the troubled relationship between Gus and his father, who was an angry, difficult person. Gus says, "He was in awe of her strength of character. Over time he felt ashamed that he hadn't earned her regard, and yet she gave it unconditionally anyway. He came to *want* her approval. He wanted to impress her. He let go of his anger, just let it go, after a lifetime of it. The children got to be with him, and we became a different family."

A pivotal moment for Gus came one day when he was yelling at his five-year-old son for not picking up his toys. Gus says that as he was ranting and accusing, he suddenly had a vision of what was happening from another perspective. He looked at the five-year-old boy and saw himself; he looked at the anxious expressions on the faces of his wife and daughter and saw his mother and sisters. He looked at himself, and saw his angry father.

Gus says that at that moment, his life changed forever. He picked up his son and held him in his arms. He knew he had to change. He also knew his own frailties and his powerful, fearful resistance to fundamental change. Facing his lifelong fear of becoming his angry and atheistic father, he began therapy, which was helpful. But he realized that for him to insure necessary change, he would have to go even deeper. Gus reversed course on his open hostility to organized religion, became a dedicated believer in God, and led his family in a faith life.

Since then, he says, he's approached everything and everyone differently. Just as his father let go of his anger, he faced his fears and let go of his own. He saw his behaviors in a different way, as cowardly, acting out of resentment, taking out his own issues on a child. Taking this turning point to heart, he refers to himself as a "recovering coward."

Gus changed his behavior. He was able to go to his family's *there* and see his actions through their eyes. What's more, at a highly emotional moment, he had the clarity to see that he was acting like a coward. And in confronting that reality, he demonstrated true courage.

■ The Power Apology

As Gus's story shows, even heroes sometimes behave badly. What separates them from other people is that they're brave enough—and humble enough—to make amends to the people they've hurt.

One of the most powerful ways to do this is what we call a "power apology." This action goes far beyond saying "I'm sorry," and as a result it can heal even the worst of wounds.

A power apology has four parts:

1. Spell out what you did or failed to do, and say, "I'm sorry and I was wrong."
2. Describe how your mistake harmed the other person. For instance, say, "I know that what I did frustrated you and made it difficult to trust and respect me. And it may take some time to earn back your trust and respect."
3. State your commitment to avoiding this mistake in the future.
4. Ask the person what you can do to make up for your mistake (beyond simply apologizing), and then do it. Most

of the time, people won't ask you to do anything, because your apology will instantly discharge the negative feelings they held toward you.

As you're reconnecting with the people you've hurt, also take a hard look at why you made each mistake in the first place. As Jim Mazzo, president of Abbott Medical Optics and senior vice president of Abbott Laboratories, told us, real influence isn't about dwelling on the negative. Instead, it's about learning from mistakes.

"I'm a baseball player," Jim says, "and I've played thousands of hours. The great coaches I've had would catch a mistake, and then have me repeat the mistake over and over until I learned *why* it doesn't work. They would break it down, step by step—for example, different ways of fielding a ground ball that won't work well."

As a result, he says, "You get it, you internalize it. Then you become much clearer about what *not* to do, and what it feels like to do the wrong thing, so you can avoid it instead of saying, 'Really? I did that?'"

So don't hide from your mistakes. Instead, as Joey Gold might say, lean *into* them. Dissect each one and figure out why you screwed up. If you can't figure it out yourself, ask other people what you're doing wrong. And if you can't break your bad habits on your own, do what Steve did: Ask your own "coaching staff"—your coworkers, your partner, your kids—to send you a clear signal when you're in danger of striking out.

While making mistakes is natural and forgivable (as long as you clean up your messes), avoiding them is a lot smarter. And one of our power influencers offered us an excellent tip for doing that: "Do nothing."

More specifically, David Wan, CEO of Harvard Business Publishing, talked about how important it is to carve out time to reflect on what you're doing right, what you might be doing wrong, and how you can do things better. If you don't fight to get that downtime into your schedule, he says, it's far too easy to put it off—and then to put it out of mind altogether.

David is a very busy man, but he's discovered the perfect time to do nothing: plane trips. When he flies to China, for instance, he'll sit back and ask himself: How are we doing as an organization? How are the people who lead our teams doing? And then he'll ask the really tough questions: How am I doing? What can I do differently to create better results?

He says, "I play back some decisions I've made, like a movie, and I watch it again. How did it play out? How could I have done it better?" Often, he realizes there are things he can do differently next time—for instance, people he can bring into the decision-making process earlier.

David says, "The airlines are rushing to put in Wi-Fi, but for me it would be better if they don't! It's helpful to have a chunk of time without those temptations and distractions to reflect, replay events, consider alternatives, and make some choices."

▶ *Usable Insight*

To err is human...to transparently own up to your error, take full responsibility, and commit to correcting it, divine.

▶ *Action Steps*

One technique used by our friend Barry Pogorel, a business consultant who's positively transformed companies around the world, is "committed conversations." In meetings, Barry asks team members to publicly make statements in this manner: "I will commit to you that ..." This is a powerful way to change people's thinking, because it holds them accountable and makes it harder for them to make excuses or dodge obligations. So here's what we'd like you to do:

1. Think of a behavior you'd like to change, and publicly say to a friend, colleague, or family member, "I will commit to you that ..." Then ask the person to hold you accountable for this commitment.

2. Think of a relationship in your life that's damaged because of something you did. Contact the person you've hurt and offer a power apology.

19

Let Gratitude Magnify
Your Influence

At times our own light goes out
and is rekindled by a spark from another person.
Each of us has cause to think with deep gratitude
of those who have lighted the flame within us.

Albert Schweitzer

Not long ago, Mark had an experience that's unusual for him. As a psychiatrist, he's used to helping other people get past negative emotions, but this time he was feeling very bad himself.

"It came on gradually," he says. "Every day, my mind started out clear, sharp, and optimistic. But by the end of each day I was dragging myself home, feeling like I was 'losing it'—confused, sorry, and just beaten down, mentally and physically."

He wondered if it was age, depression, or something worse. But instinctively, he knew there was a different explanation. Finally, after another brutal day, he found the answer.

"What I realized," he says, "was that every day, in almost every conversation, I dealt with people who were extremely disappointed in life or other people or extremely disappointed in themselves. Because I listen in a way that causes people to 'feel felt' by me, I'd finish every day feeling filled up with all the frustration, disappointment, hurt, anger, and fear I'd felt with people each day."

Mark realized that he couldn't influence other people in positive ways if he felt so bad himself. And he also realized that the fix for his problem couldn't come from outside. It had to come from him.

So he did something very simple: He sat down and wrote a list of all the people he's grateful to in life—especially the ones who believed in him when he didn't, and those who went to bat for him when he couldn't speak up for himself. And after he composed the long list, remembering the acts of caring by these individuals and letting his gratitude toward them wash over him, he was literally unable to remember or experience any disappointment or frustration with anything or anyone in his life.

Mark was able to diagnose and overcome his problem quickly because as a psychiatrist, he's seen others trapped in the same vicious cycle. These people were giving their all and getting negativity in return. So they found themselves responding negatively as well: with apathy, confusion, anger, or disappointment. And in return, the world gave them more of the same.

Gratitude breaks this cycle—instantly. In place of a vicious cycle, an appreciative cycle occurs. Each time we go through that appreciative cycle, it accelerates like a cyclotron of good karma. Earlier in this book, we talked about offering a power thank-you as a gift to another person. But expressing gratitude is also a gift to yourself. When you do this, you won't simply feel better. You'll also find yourself exerting a more powerful and positive influence on the people around you, and they will spread that positive influence to others.

In fact, gratitude is one of the themes we heard most often from our group of power influencers. Over and over, they looked for ways to tell us about the people who'd supported, stood up for, and looked out for them. Here are some of the stories they shared.

▪ Appreciating a Mentor

A while ago, Mark saw a flattering article in the *New York Times* about Jim Sinegal, the cofounder and former CEO of Costco, the leading warehouse club chain and also one of the largest retailers in the United States. Mark sent Jim a message complimenting him on his achievements at Costco and asking if he could write an article about Jim for another publication.

Jim phoned Mark in response, but to Mark's surprise, Jim called because he was upset.

Jim explained how unhappy he was about the article, because it gave him too much credit. He thought the credit should go to Sol Price, founder of Price Club, a forerunner of Costco. Jim felt very strongly that Costco's success was Sol's story, because Sol believed in him, gave him his chance, and supported him afterward.

Jim doesn't have an Ivy League pedigree. He thinks of himself as a former "juvenile delinquent" who could easily have gone in the wrong direction if he hadn't had Sol Price as a mentor.

Sol pioneered the warehouse retail store concept with Price Club, and Jim learned more from him than how to run a company. He learned how to value everyone a company touches—from customers to employees to vendors to shareholders. Jim learned that if you take advantage of opportunity, you don't have to take advantage of people.

In 1995, Costco merged with Price Club and acquired the "do well by doing good" spirit of Sol Price. Sol lives on through Jim, who has served as a director on the Costco board since its founding and continues to draw upon Sol's positive influence.

To sum it up, Jim says: "Gratitude is the key to the right attitude. First, you're grateful that you had the opportunity to work, learn, and observe from someone for whom you have so much respect.

That respect and gratitude cause you to reflect upon any important decision, and to ask yourself 'how would he or she react in this situation?' Most likely, that question will guide you in the search for the right answer. By making the correct choice and doing the right thing, you honor your mentor."

As Jim Sinegal notes, "gratitude is the right attitude" because it encourages you to act in ways that enhance your relationships and reputation. And focusing actively on gratitude is even more crucial during the bad times in your life.

Earlier, we talked about influencing under adversity. At moments like this, gratitude is a powerful ally because, when you're focused on what you're grateful for, you spend less time thinking about what's wrong in your life and more time thinking about what's right. And this attitude draws people toward you rather than driving them away.

Bill Childs, an information technology pioneer who helped build some of the first healthcare information systems at Lockheed, offered us a firsthand example recently.

Bill is seventy-one years old, and just before we spoke with him, he'd come from the doctor after receiving the news that he would need surgery on his hand and wrist. He was getting off a bus in Orlando, and the bus driver forgot to put the stair down. When Bill stepped forward with no stair to catch his foot, he fell headlong onto the concrete. He fell so hard he shattered his wrist, and over fifty pieces of bone needed to be picked out.

Regardless, when he spoke to us, he was in an incurably sunny mood. All he could talk about was how blessed and fortunate he was—fortunate the injury wasn't much worse; fortunate to have had such a long, rewarding career and fifty-year marriage; fortunate to be able to help people; and fortunate to have more time left to keep helping.

By the time we finished our conversation with him, we felt inspired and uplifted. And we felt grateful for the reminder that it's possible to influence positively—and powerfully—even when life isn't going the way we've planned.

■ Thanking a Legend

Ken Blanchard is one of the most influential management writers and consultants of our era. He's coauthored over thirty best-selling books and is best known for *The One Minute Manager*, which has sold over thirteen million copies and been translated into thirty-seven languages. Here's his story about two people who left him and his wife Margie filled with gratitude:

In 1985 I got a call from Larry Hughes, president of William Morrow, asking me if I'd consider writing a book with Norman Vincent Peale. My first response was, "Is he still alive?" My parents had gone to Peale's church before I was born. Larry said, "Not only is he alive; he's an incredible human being—and so is his wife." That summer I flew to New York and had a three-hour lunch with Norman, Ruth, and Larry. Margie didn't make it to that meeting.

We were advised by a friend one time that if you're going to work with somebody, you need to consider two things: essence and form. Essence means heart-to-heart and values-to-values. Form means "how are you going to do it?" During that three-hour lunch, Norman and Ruth didn't talk about form at all. It was all about essence—who they were and who Margie and I were.

My initial thought was to write a book on the power of positive management. But Larry Hughes thought that the country was in desperate need of a good book on ethics. At the end of the lunch, Norman asked Ruth the ultimate essence question: "Ruth, should we write this book with this young man?" (I was forty-six at the time, and they were forty years older.) Her answer was, "Absolutely—under one condition. From now on, whenever we meet, Margie will come, too. The four of us will work on this together."

We learned so many transformational things from Norman and Ruth.

First, we learned how important it is to be a team when you're married. We observed that they each had their strength areas and didn't try to tell the other one what to do. Very much like us, Ruth was the one who made sure things happened and Norman was the idea person.

Every morning Norman and Ruth would take a two-mile walk together, holding hands, but they wouldn't talk. They called it their "alone time together." So when it comes to the teamwork of marriage, they were a great example to us.

Second, we learned that if you keep your sense of humor and a positive attitude, as you get older, you get cuter! They were so cute. Now that we're getting older, we're concentrating on being cuter.

Third, we learned what a powerful motivator learning is. We saw how excited they were to get up every day, because they never knew what they might learn that day.

Last but not least, they taught us about the power of spirituality. Margie and I were not believers when we met Norman and Ruth, but through their loving encouragement, we started to look at our own spirituality. Now spirituality is a major part of our life.

Norman died quietly in his sleep on Christmas Eve at 95, and Ruth died at 101. Right to the end, both of them were vibrant and ready to go.

I probably didn't express to Norman how much he meant to me, although I think I reminded him whenever I talked to him. But I did write a book on my spiritual journey in which I acknowledged Norman for his role in my spiritual growth. I finished it on the twenty-second of December, when Norman was quite sick. I overnighted it to him. Ruth took it into him on the twenty-fourth of December and said, "Norman,

look what Ken sent you. And he dedicated the book to you." She said
that he may already have left his body, but she believed he knew. He
died later that night."

Ken and Margie's time with the Peales was a turning point
in their life, inspiring them to add a spiritual dimension to their
training and leadership development services. As a result, they're
touching thousands of people on an even deeper level—and, in the
process, they're paying forward their debt of gratitude to Norman
and Ruth Peale.

———

Like Jim Sinegal and Ken Blanchard, dozens of influencers eagerly
shared their stories about people who'd helped them advance in
their careers and become better people. These stories touched us
deeply, but they did much more than that: They made us feel grateful to the people who shared them with us.

Interestingly, there's even a scientific reason for this. It's called
"mirroring." Scientists now know that the human brain contains
"mirror neurons"—specialized cells that cause us to respond to
other people's actions and emotions as if we're experiencing them
ourselves.

Thus, when you perform an act of gratitude—whether you're
thanking a person directly or talking about someone else who's
helped you—the person who's listening to you feels a strong sense
of gratitude as well. And that immediately creates a stronger bond
between the two of you.

So if you want to magnify your influence, share your appreciation whenever you can. Go out of your way to thank the people
who help you, and tell other people about their kind acts. Create a
mental habit of being thankful every day. Focus your energy not on
being angry at the people who've hurt you, but on being grateful

toward the people who've supported you. And if you find yourself trapped in a cycle of negativity, actively break out of it and start a brand-new cycle of appreciation instead.

▶ *Usable Insight*
You can focus on being grateful or disappointed. The choice is yours.

▶ *Action Steps*
1. Before the end of this week, tell at least five people to whom you're grateful why you are grateful to them.
2. The next time you're feeling weighed down by negative comments or experiences at work or at home, immediately think of three people to whom you are grateful and mentally review the things they did on your behalf.

SECTION 7

Putting It All Together

Now that you've mastered each step of connected influence, it's time to put them all together. In the following case studies, we'll look at four very different scenarios—a hospital disaster drill, a struggling marriage, a warring group, and a freeway dog rescue—and see how our influencers pulled off their great outcomes.

20

Case Study #1—
A Fuzzy Rescue

▪ Envisioning a Great Outcome: "No Pet Left Behind"

Sheila Choi has been going for great outcomes since 2005 when she started a nonprofit organization, The Fuzzy Pet Foundation. Her foundation is dedicated to eliminating pet overpopulation via spaying and neutering and rescue services. She's motivated by the fact that four to five million healthy and adoptable dogs and cats are killed every year in the United States.

Sheila's chosen to focus her foundation's efforts on the most difficult cases: the animals that are most in need and least likely to be adopted. Fuzzy Pet takes in the cases others often avoid—animals with broken bones or missing limbs, or animals that have been abused or left to starve.

Sheila has made a personal commitment to never say no to an animal in need. Her passion inspires an all-volunteer force of people who give their free time and even schedule vacations around the animals.

▪ Seeing Past a Blind Spot: "Just Call Animal Control"

If a cat is injured or a dog is running on the freeway, most people call the police or animal control. But Sheila knows what really happens in these cases, because she's taken the time to go to the ***their there*** of these agencies. She knows that calling 911 won't work because, with good reason, emergency services prioritize human emergencies. She also knows that in many cases, animal control simply can't respond quickly enough.

When a dog is on the freeway, therefore, she's the one who gets out and does something about it.

Here's an example. In January, 2010, after a late night meeting for her foundation in downtown Los Angeles, Sheila missed the entrance to the freeway in East Los Angeles and made a quick turn into a dark alley to come back around. Her headlights were bright, and right in front of her car she saw a white, medium-sized dog sleeping in the middle of the road.

She immediately braked her car. It was a rough-looking neighborhood and she was alone, but she decided to act. She put on her emergency headlights, parked in the middle of the road, and stepped out of her car in high heels.

▪ Engaging in *Their There*: Going to a Dog's Perspective

At that point, Sheila also saw a brown dog who appeared to be protecting the white dog sleeping in the middle of the road. The white dog was in desperate need, and probably would have died or been killed by a car if Sheila had not intervened.

The brown dog let out a protective growl when Sheila approached the white dog. Both dogs were dirty and seemed to have been neglected for a long time. They had matted fur and they were both very scared and wary of her.

Sheila saw a young man walking nearby, and she asked about the dogs. He replied, "Dunno, they live on the streets. They're street dogs." She asked him to help, but he declined. "They aren't my dogs. They just live here."

She had no one to help, no one to call at that hour, and nowhere to take them. She was also concerned that they might flee out of fear at any moment.

She quickly walked over to her car and found a couple of emergency leashes. Under her car seat were a bag of dog snack crumbs and a can of wet kitty food. (You can tell she's always prepared for a great outcome.)

It took about thirty minutes to lure in the dogs, but both came to her eventually because they were starving. Each dog would take one step, grab a treat, and then scurry away. Eventually, she was able to get an emergency leash around each animal and push both dogs into her car.

By then it was almost 3:00 AM, and Sheila needed to find some temporary shelter for the dogs. She called her veterinary technician, who works at her local vet's office. Luckily, the tech answered the phone. Sheila begged her, saying she desperately needed temporary shelter for the dogs. She feared that taking them to the local pound would be a death sentence for them.

The technician reluctantly consented. They met in the parking lot of the vet's office and opened the doors at 3:45 AM. Both dogs were boarded at the vet's office, examined, vaccinated, and treated for fleas.

■ Doing More . . . Sheila Style

When it came to the white dog, the veterinarian called Sheila to say she needed to be picked up. She was a "fear-biter," and wouldn't allow the vet near her. The vet couldn't spay her, although he was able to treat the brown dog with ease. None of the other vet techs were able to handle the white dog.

The vet was on the phone with Sheila for about forty-five minutes explaining that the white dog was not adoptable due to her fear-induced aggression. He recommended euthanasia.

Sheila rushed over and asked if she could handle the white dog on her own. The vet rolled his eyes and told her the dog would resort to biting. He told Sheila to go in the kennel area at her own risk, and he warned her that he wouldn't be responsible if she was bitten.

Sheila went to the back area with canned food. She was gentle with the white dog, who seemed to recognize her. The dog wagged her tail and then cowered, trying to hide in the corner of her cage. Sheila attempted to put a muzzle on her, but the dog was too fast. So Sheila tossed in some food. The dog would inch closer, then back off when Sheila tried to touch her.

After about an hour or so, she crawled over to Sheila's side. Sheila petted her, rubbed her tummy, and talked to her. At last she finally held the dog in her arms and was able to bring her over to the vet. Sheila continued to hold her on the treatment table while she was anesthetized and then spayed.

These stories don't always have happy endings, but this one did. With the help of Sheila's rescue network, both dogs were placed in loving homes.

Saving animals is Sheila's cause, but she can't do it alone. And she doesn't need to, because rescues like these tell people that she's serious about her motto: "No Pet Left Behind." Because of her powerful reputation, both volunteers and celebrities flock to her cause. And every year, The Fuzzy Pet Foundation saves, rehabilitates, and "re-homes" nearly two hundred cats and dogs.

21

Case Study #2—
Everything Matters

■ Envisioning a Great Outcome: "One Patient at a Time"

Stanford is one of the top medical centers and universities in the world. But Amir Rubin, president and CEO of Stanford Hospital and Clinics, says, "We have great ambitions for improving what we do even more."

He explains, "We don't want to just serve people locally, but the world. Our people, institutions, and resources give us that opportunity."

Rubin says it starts with their mission as an organization: "Heal humanity through science and compassion one patient at a time."

Those last five words—*one patient at a time*—make a huge difference. They require a commitment to *every single person* who receives care at Stanford. That's amazing.

■ Seeing Past the Blind Spot: "Our Reputation Is Good Enough Already"

Many institutions build an amazing reputation and then sit on it for decades. That's because they're in their blind spot ("We're already successful, so we must be doing well enough").

Stanford isn't one of these places. They don't look at their work from their own point of view. They look at it from each patient's point of view, and, because of their global stature, from the entire world's point of view.

Rubin says, "This is not a place to coast or to get by on the strength of our brand or reputation. This is a place to do great things. We've made a commitment to society to do great things."

Rubin explains that when you get serious about committing to the goal of "every patient, every day," everything suddenly matters. Every person, every job, every part of the facility from the operating rooms to the parking lots—*everything* matters.

■ Engaging Patients *and* Employees in *Their There*

For Rubin, going for great outcomes at Stanford involves engaging everyone in the organization.

As he points out, "The actions we take to get from Monday to Tuesday, then Tuesday to Wednesday, and so on, define the culture." In other words, *every action by every employee matters—and every employee's viewpoint is important.*

At Stanford, leadership teams engage directly with staff and patients. They're connected, involved, and accountable for making it work. Everyone has a personal stake in creating a great outcome for every individual patient—no exceptions. On a regular basis, groups "huddle" to share best practices, ideas, and feedback.

Rubin notes that you can't make this happen without making an organization a great place to work. So while employees focus on "one patient at a time," managers focus on another great outcome—"one employee at a time."

■ Doing More . . . Stanford Style

Stanford's commitment to every patient leads their staff to constantly look for ways to make their standard of care even better.

For example, Stanford frequently performs drills to prepare them to respond to a natural disaster. The challenge in this scenario isn't just about dealing with people who are ill. In addition, you need to figure out how to deal with the "worried well"—people who are afraid they might have the illness even though they don't. These people can create an intake logjam that blocks people who really need treatment from getting it.

In response to this problem, two Stanford physicians—Eric Weiss and Gregory Gilbert—came up with a creative idea: a drive-through triage. The idea took hold when Weiss, traveling with his family, pulled into a McDonald's parking lot and saw customers coughing in the restaurant.

Rather than having overwhelming numbers of people jam up the emergency facility, Weiss and Gilbert proposed they would take the medical team into the parking lot. The team could take vital signs and assess people very quickly in their cars, identifying who was really sick and who simply needed reassurance.

The physicians designed and successfully tested this innovative drive-through screening and treatment process. It increases efficiency, reduces cross-contamination, lowers costs, treats patients more effectively, and enables the staff to focus their efforts where they can do the most good. And just as important, it treats one patient at a time—easing the fears of the worried well while quickly getting sick people the care they need.

That's a great outcome that resulted from a culture that focuses on generating them. And it's one of the reasons why year after year, patients rank Stanford as one of the best hospitals in the world.

22

Case Study #3—
Poised for Life

■ Envisioning a Great Outcome: "Nature and Nurture Are Just Two Strikes"

A high-powered couple had a great outcome: They wanted to give their marriage one more chance after they'd separated.

So they came to Mark, who was providing clinical therapy for families at the time. Mark is one of the world's leading experts on helping divorced couples successfully remarry their ex-spouses through his Recoupling Therapy.

"Did you know that children get their mannerisms from either or both parents, but get their sense of well-being and security from how their parents deal with conflict between each other?" Mark asked.

This couple hadn't yet gone past the point of no return. But still, when they heard Mark's observation about children, both parents agreed with a chuckle, "Well, looks like our kids are screwed." They went on to describe their families' problems with depression, bipolar illness, and alcohol and substance abuse, and to talk about how they grew up in chaotic homes filled with abuse, guilt-tripping, and manipulation.

Mark asked them, "What if you could reach a point one year down the road where you each looked at each other and said, 'Not only did we make it work, we successfully created the happy and healthy home that neither of us had, and our kids are thriving'?"

Again in unison they replied, "Nah, that's not possible. We're both too messed up."

Mark replied, "Nature and nurture are just two strikes. You still have one more chance."

■ Seeing Past the Blind Spot: "Blind and Infantile"

Mark asked the couple, "Would you agree that when you see people with poise under pressure that you greatly admire and respect them and would even like to be like them?"

Both responded, "Yes."

"And," Mark continued, "would you also agree that when people act in an infantile, hostile, sniping way, it's really ugly and embarrassing to see and be around?"

Again the answer from them came, "Yes."

■ Engaging in *Their There*

Mark asked, "Would you agree that every day things happen that upset, frustrate, anger, and disappoint you either in others or in yourself?"

"Of course," they both responded.

"Then tell me if you agree with this observation about other people's and your personalities," Mark explained. "I think there are three concentric circles to your personalities. Every time something upsetting happens or someone does something upsetting to you, it triggers in the innermost circle an unforgiving streak in you. If you don't manage or deal with that streak and it overtakes the rest of your personality, you will end up bitter. All bitter people are one hundred percent dyed-in-the-wool unforgiving."

He added, "When that unforgiving streak bubbles over like boiling water, it crosses over into the second concentric circle that's the retaliatory streak in your personality. If you don't manage that area it leads to constant fighting and conflict, which is what caused you to separate.

"And finally," he said, "if *that* bubbles over, it crosses into the final concentric circle, which is the distrustful streak in your personality. If you don't manage that, then you become emotionally estranged as if you don't even know the person any more."

Both spouses were actually looking up into their minds' eyes as Mark spoke, and he could tell that what he was describing was exactly what had occurred with them. Their unforgiving, retaliatory, and distrustful streaks were what had destroyed their relationship—all streaks fueled by their genes and their upbringing.

■ Doing More . . . "From Enemies to Sponsors"

"So here's the deal," Mark said. "When either of you becomes frustrated, disappointed, or upset, you give in to your impulse to blame and retaliate. Then it builds into a corrosive distrust that's rotted the warm feelings you once had for each other. To a great extent you have each become addicted to that behavior, and when you each or both act with it, you destroy another piece of your relationship." They nodded.

"So every day, or as they say in Twelve-Step Programs, 'one day at a time,' you will each focus on feeling your upset, disappointment, frustration, and anger, but then not act on it. At the end of each day you will share the story of an impulse you didn't give in to. Those can include not yelling at one of the children when they are whining in the car or not giving in to road rage if someone cuts you off. And you will root each other on. Over time, you will begin to become emotionally strong and tough and your self-respect will increase because you are acting in a classy instead of an infantile way."

What Mark has noticed with couples who follow this approach and practice it on a "one day at a time" basis—and he no longer sees couples who won't—is that after eight weeks, a significant number will say they are better as couples than they ever have been. After the next eight weeks, they will say that they're better as individuals than they have ever been. And after the last eight weeks, they will say that other couples are noticing a very positive difference and are asking them what happened. A few couples have responded with true humility: "We decided to grow up."

Instead of being the couples headed directly for a messy divorce, a number of these couples have become admired role models in their circle of friends. And this husband and wife, who started with two strikes against them, are in that elite group.

23

Case Study #4—Taming a Temperamental Group

▪ Envisioning a Great Outcome: Getting Feuding People Back on the Same Page

Ivan Misner, dubbed the "father of modern networking" by CNN, runs BNI, the largest business networking organization in the world. BNI has over six thousand chapters around the world, and last year its members referred 6.5 million clients. It's a huge success, creating lifelong friendships as well as billions of dollars in referrals.

But sometimes, as with any organization, tensions start running high in a BNI chapter. When that happens, Ivan is sometimes the one who steps in to turn things around.

▪ The Blind Spot: We Need to Talk About What's *Wrong*

To transform a group of antagonistic people into allies, Ivan uses an approach he calls the "solutions focus technique," which he learned from Dr. Mark McKergow. Here's how it works.

Misner says, "Let's say you have a group of people who are upset with the quality of referrals. The first step is to ask: 'On a scale of one to ten, where one means not one single referral is good and ten equals 'I can't imagine better referrals,' how bad is the problem?"

People almost always say three or four. And that's when Ivan shocks them by saying, "You think it's three? Why so high?"

His question knocks them for a loop because they feel like it's a low score. And with that question, Ivan resets their mind-set so they're ready to ask, "How do we add value?" instead of asking, "What is subtracting value?"

Misner says, "What you're doing with this technique is focusing on what's going right, and building on that. When you focus on what's wrong, you become an expert on doing what's wrong. It's human nature that complaints can lead to more complaints, and there are always some people who complain like it's an Olympic event. Their idea of fixing a problem is to stop doing what's wrong, but that doesn't fix it. We can get sucked into that. Instead, it takes redirecting attention and effort toward solution steps."

■ Engaging in *Their There*

Once Ivan refocuses his group, he's ready to engage them. But he doesn't simply come from **his here** and offer a list of solutions. Instead, he goes to one person who's named a score, repeats the score, and asks, "What's one thing that would make it a four instead of a three?"

Typically, the person says something like, "When someone gives me a referral, he should let the referral know I'm calling first. If everyone did that, our referrals would be better." Or maybe the person says, "People should tell me more about the referral. They shouldn't just give me a name and number."

Ivan writes the person's answer on a whiteboard and then asks another person and writes that answer down, too. Then he asks someone else, and so on, until everyone has a chance to be heard.

■ Doing More by Letting Others Add Value

At this point, Ivan could do more by telling people how they should implement their suggestions. But he doesn't. That's because one of his favorite philosophies is, "Don't 'shoulda' on people. Don't say, 'You shoulda done this' or 'Your group shoulda done that.'" This approach, he says, creates resistance and defensiveness.

So instead, Ivan encourages other people in the group to elaborate on their ideas. And when he does contribute a thought, he offers it with humility. He asks, "Are you open to some ideas?" or says, "That inspires a couple thoughts. Would you like to hear them, to see if there's anything that might be useful?"

He says, "You coach and guide them, but they don't feel like you *told* them to do anything. You're helping them see that they already *know* what it will take to make this a ten. They've got the answers at hand." It's a respectful approach, and an empowering one. And by "strategically getting out of the way," Misner takes these groups to a whole new level of cooperation and success.

Tell Us About Your Great Outcomes!

The secret of getting ahead is getting started.
Mark Twain

All this will not be finished in the first one hundred days. Nor will it be finished
in the first one thousand days, not in the life of this administration,
nor even perhaps in our lifetime on this planet. But let us begin.
John F. Kennedy, in his inaugural address as president of the United States

We're inspired by the influencers we've worked with over the years, and by all the people whose stories you've read in this book. And we're inspired by everyone who achieves a great outcome through genuine connected influence, not manipulation and deceit.

When you do this, or when you see others doing it, we'd love to hear about it and help spread the word.

We want to keep shining a light on people who are influencing by example, so we can all take inspiration from them. If you have examples of how people are using the power of positive influence, please let us know at www.GoInfluenceNow.com so we can keep paying it forward.

Thank you!

ACKNOWLEDGMENTS

This book comes from the contributions of many wonderful people.

First, we're both blessed to have people in our lives whose presence and love give special meaning to this book and everything we do.

Mark is deeply grateful to the beloved people who continue to influence him and to whom he can turn to when he needs a boost of inspiration. In body: Noel Goulston, Robert Goulston, Lisa Stotsky Goulston, Lauren Goulston, Emily Goulston, Billy Goulston, Michael Stotsky, Warren Bennis, Bob Eckert, Bill Liao, Devan Capur, Lt. General Marty Steele, Colonel Tom Tyrrell, Keith Minella, Scott Adelson, Jim Freedman, David Herman, Gordon Gregory, Chris Beveridge, Lee Ryan, Pete Lakey, Deb Boelkes, Genevieve Chase, Joan Lynch, Rebecca Torrey, Pete Linnett, Doug Linnett, Bronywn Fryer, Pam Golum, Peter Winick, Marhnelle and Dave Hibbard. And in spirit: Ruth and Irving Goulston, William McNary, Edwin Shneidman, Al Dorskind, Ken Florence, Ward Wiedman, Walter Dunn, Herbert Linden, and Ray Tye.

John wants to acknowledge the core group of loved ones who for many years always have held him close, no matter what. Their unconditional support and leadership in his life provide inspiring reminders of the kind of person he aspires to be: Mary Ullmen, John Joseph Ullmen, Karen Ullmen, Jim Adcox, Sam Culbert, Stephanie Kagimoto, Maurice Monette, Ron & Alexandra Seigel, and James P. Sullivan, Jr.

We're thankful for the terrific team at AMACOM books who have supported this project through every stage, led by Executive Editor Ellen Kadin.

Thanks also to Bill Gladstone, our excellent agent at Waterside Productions, who set the stage for us to turn our plan into reality.

Alison Blake's wisdom and grace have been indispensable on this journey. She always helps us find our voice and balance. She is the calm and compass in the storm.

We're both aware that the "work" we do is a privilege, and we're honored by the trust our clients place in us. Therefore, we want to give special thanks and acknowledgment to those who teach us, challenge us, and give us the gift of partnering with them to make a difference in their lives and ours.

We're grateful also to those who have shared their stories, insights and perspectives with us for this project: Calvin Abe, Brian Adams, Anthony Allman, Michael Altman, David Applebaum, Alex Banayan, Bill Barber, Glen Barros, Giang Biscan, Brian Bishop, Meredith Blake, Ken Blanchard, David Booth, David Bradford, Nachum Braverman, Steve Brooks, Adam Carolla, Giselle Chapman, Bill Childs, Sheila Choi, Jim Clark, Larry Clark, Beth Comstock, Ana Corrales, Geoff Cowan, Mike Critelli, Mike Devlin, Bob Dorsch, Jim Downing, Brad Feld, Keith Ferrazzi, Jonathan Fielding, Bob Fiske, Jonathan Fitzgarrald, Christa Foley, Mary Fox, Danny Friedland, Reggie Gilyard, Joey Gold, Marshall Goldsmith, Betty Gonzalez-Morkos, Mike Grier, Katalina Groh, Peter Guber, Mel Hall, David Heinemeier Hansson, Tony Hsieh, Mark Homan, Jeff Jackson, Andy Johnson, Gus Lee, Lyle Kellman, Hank Kennedy, Colleen Kohlsaat, Robin Kramer, David Labistour, Risa Lavizzo-Mourey, Mark Lefko, David Levinson, Jeanine Martin, Mike Martinez, Eric Marton, Jim Mazzo, Karen Miles, Ivan Misner, Rick Moran, Kouji Nakata, Parisa Naseralavi, Raymond Nourmand, Richard Otte, Ron Paxton, Barry Pogorel, Dwayne Proctor, Debbie Quintana, John Rawling, Dennis Robbins, Amy Roberts, Marchelle Roberts, Heidi Roizen, Alison Rosen, Ivan Rosenberg, Amir Rubin, Gina Rudan, Glenn Rupert, Karen Salmansohn, Carla Sanger, Jim Schroer, Kathryn Shulz, Greg

Scott, Larry Senn, Deborah Shames, Casey Sheahan, Jim Sinegal, Lou Sokolovsky, Anthony Sola, Vikki Stone, Stefan Swanepoel, Pat Sweeney, Marilyn Tam, George Vardakas, Dave Vucina, David Wan, Josh Webster, Ernie Wilson, Renard Wright, and Jay Young.

And for you our readers, we'd like to close by giving *you* a power thank you. We know your time is precious to you. Thank you for making time to read our book. We hope what we've learned and shared helps you develop more REAL INFLUENCE to enhance your career and your life. Your investment in us motivates us to be of further service to you, and we welcome your feedback.

INDEX

ABOUT THE AUTHORS

Mark Goulston, MD, is a business psychiatrist, consultant, chairman and cofounder of Heartfelt Leadership, and the author of *Just Listen*, *Get Out of Your Own Way*, and *Get Out of Your Own Way at Work*. He also writes a syndicated career column for Tribune Media Services; blogs for *Fast Company*, *Business Insider*, *Huffington Post*, and *Psychology Today*; and is featured frequently in major media, including *The Wall Street Journal*, *Harvard Business Review*, *Fortune*, *Newsweek*, CNN, NPR, and Fox News. He lives in Los Angeles.

John Ullmen, Ph.D., is an acclaimed executive coach whose clients include dozens of leading international firms. He oversees MotivationRules.com, conducts popular feedback-based seminars on influence in organizations, and teaches at the UCLA Anderson School of Management.